COLORING FLOWERS

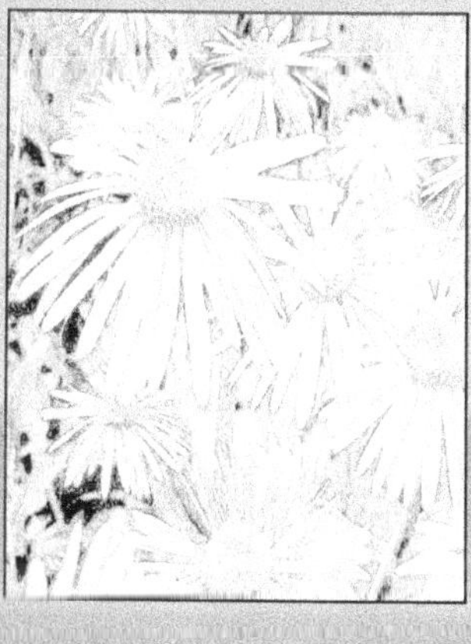
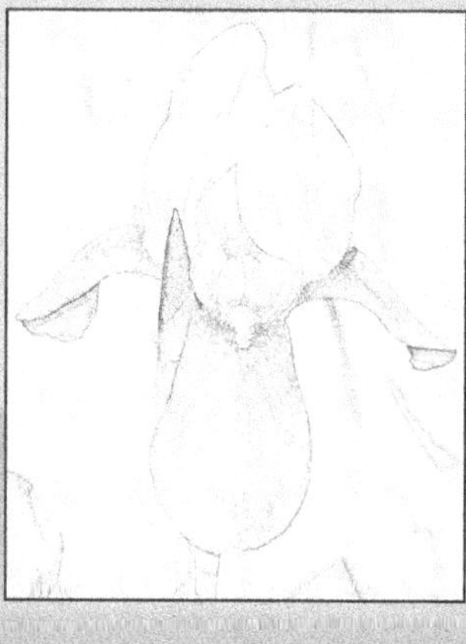
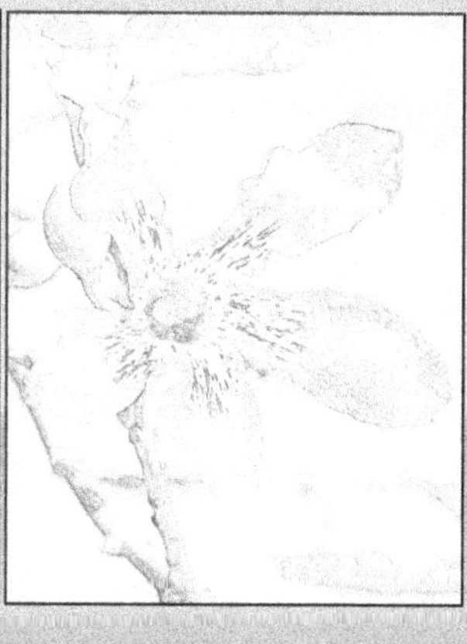
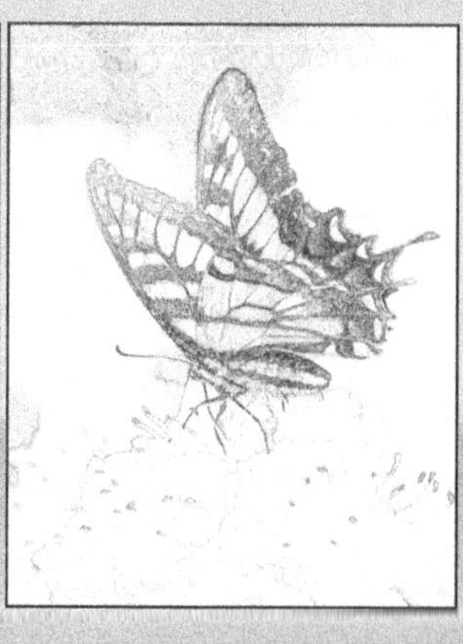
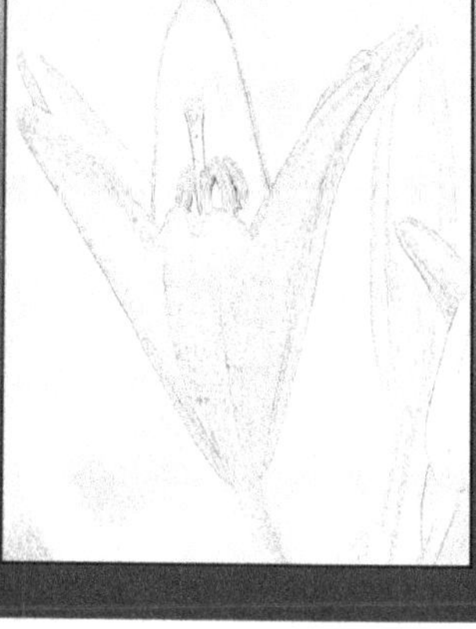
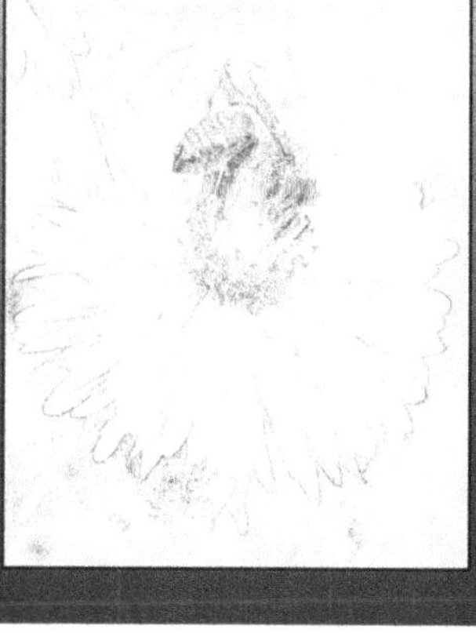
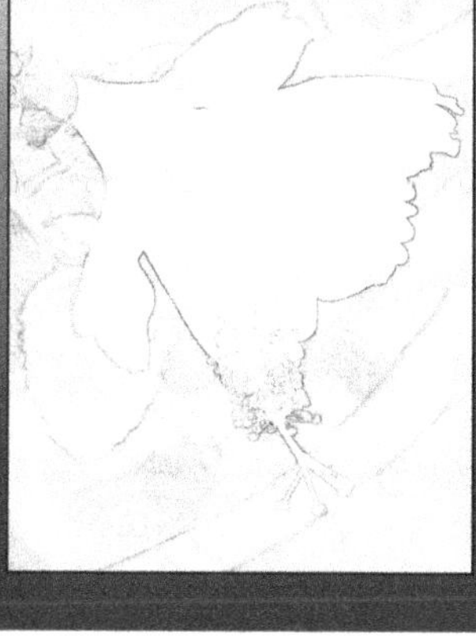
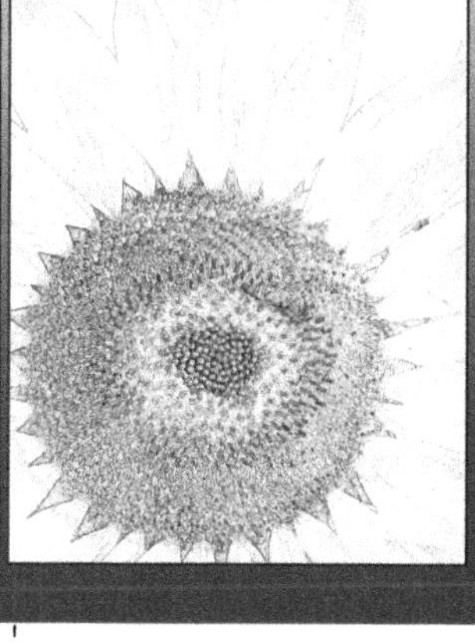

Coloring Flowers

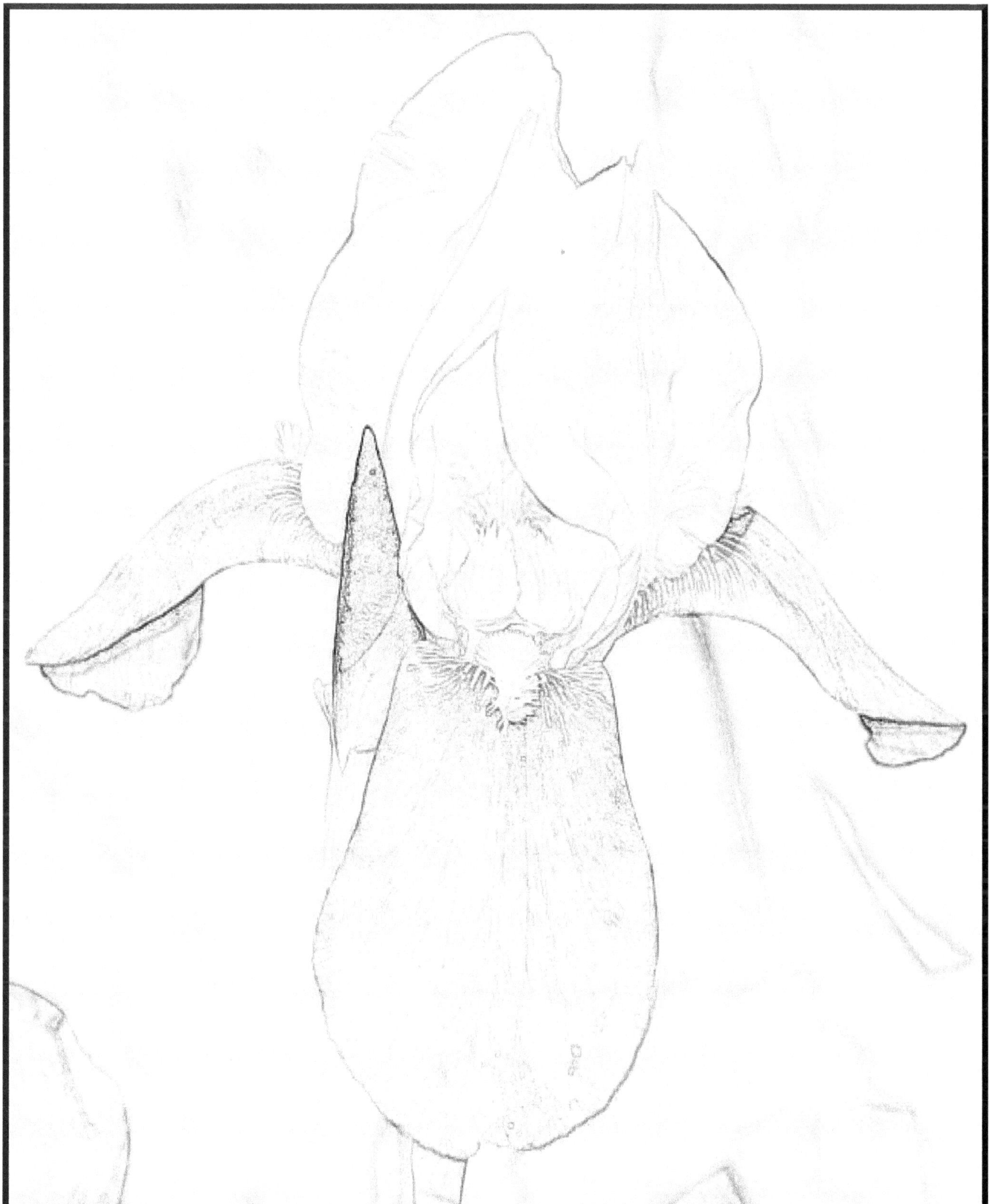

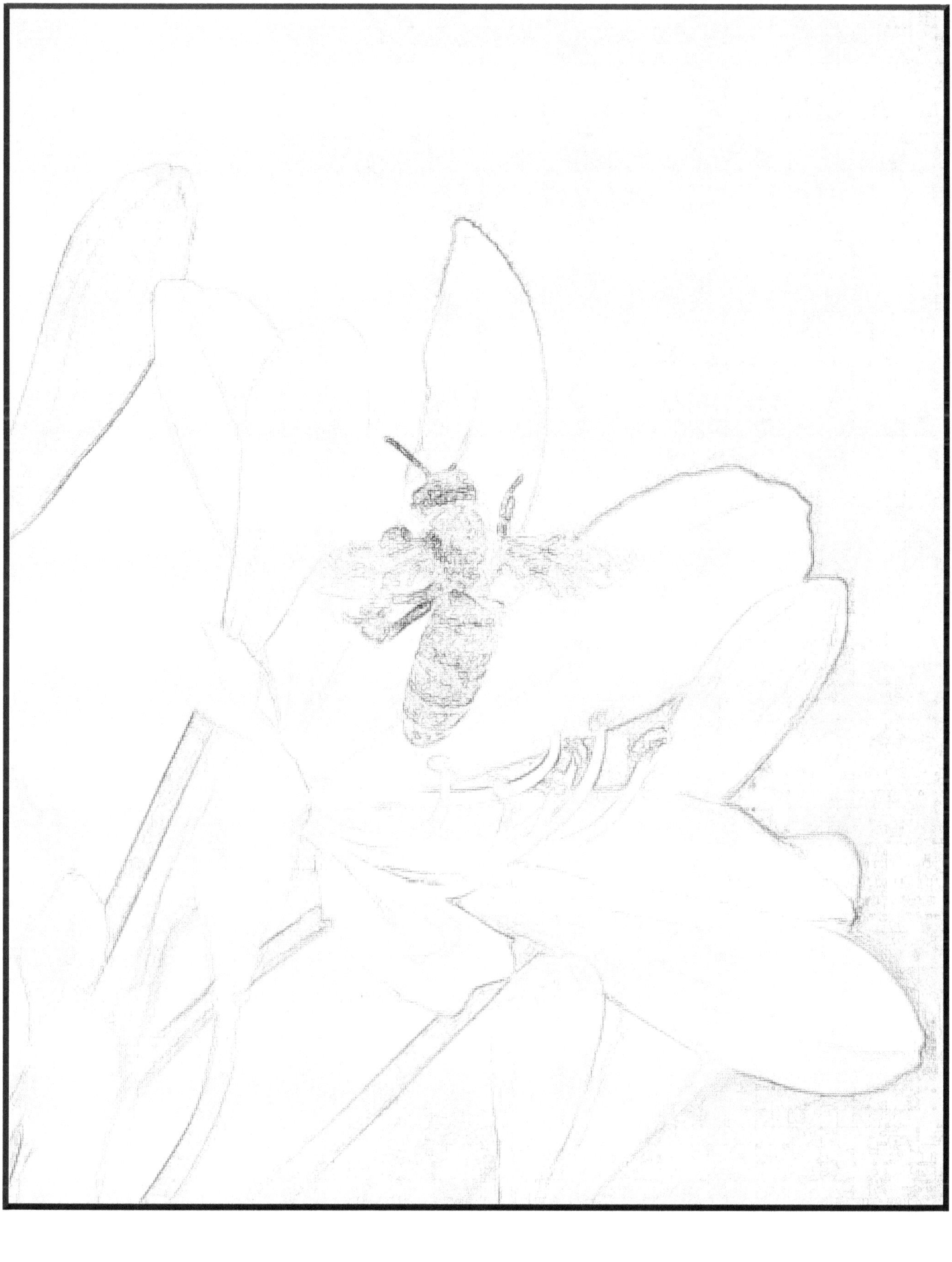

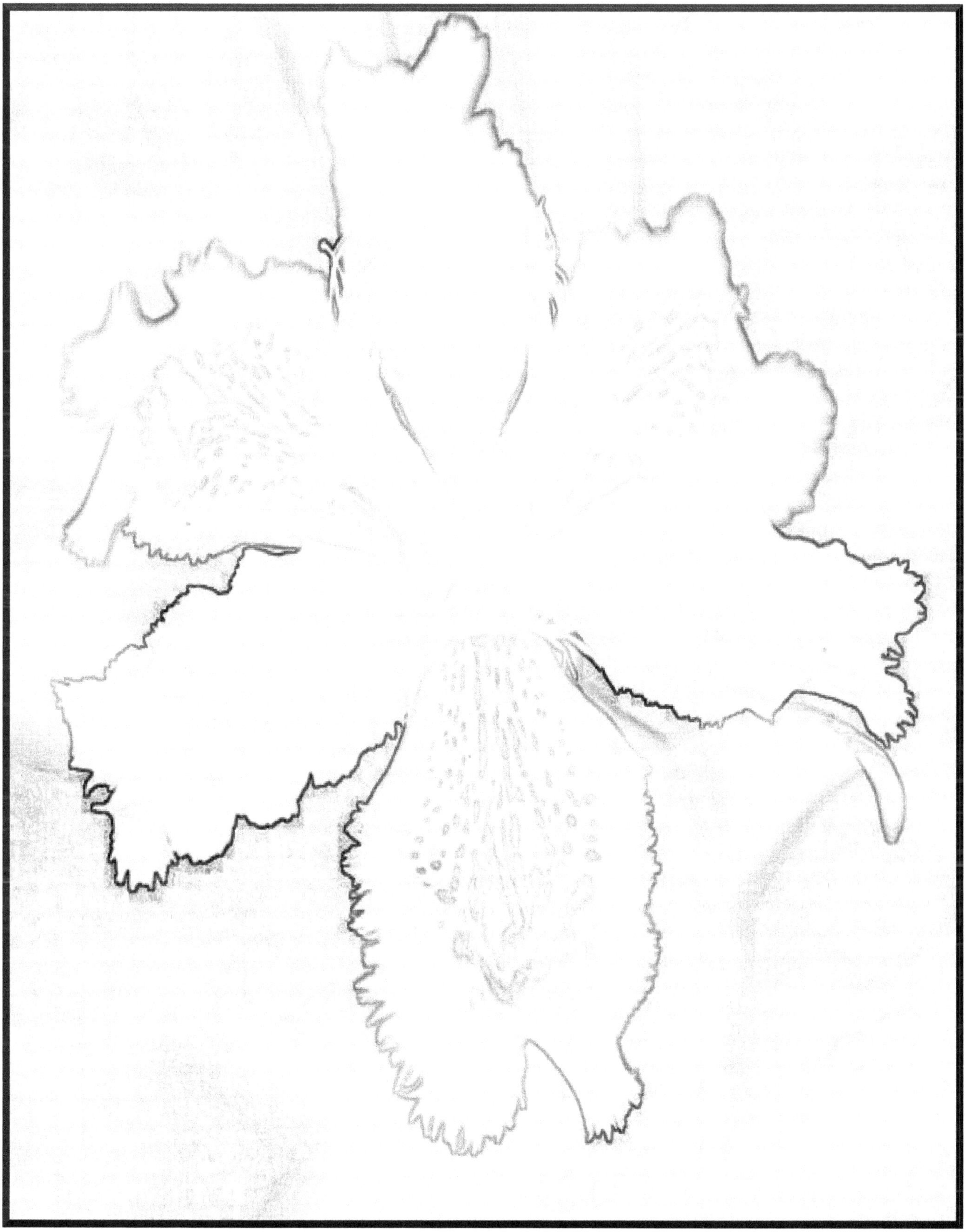

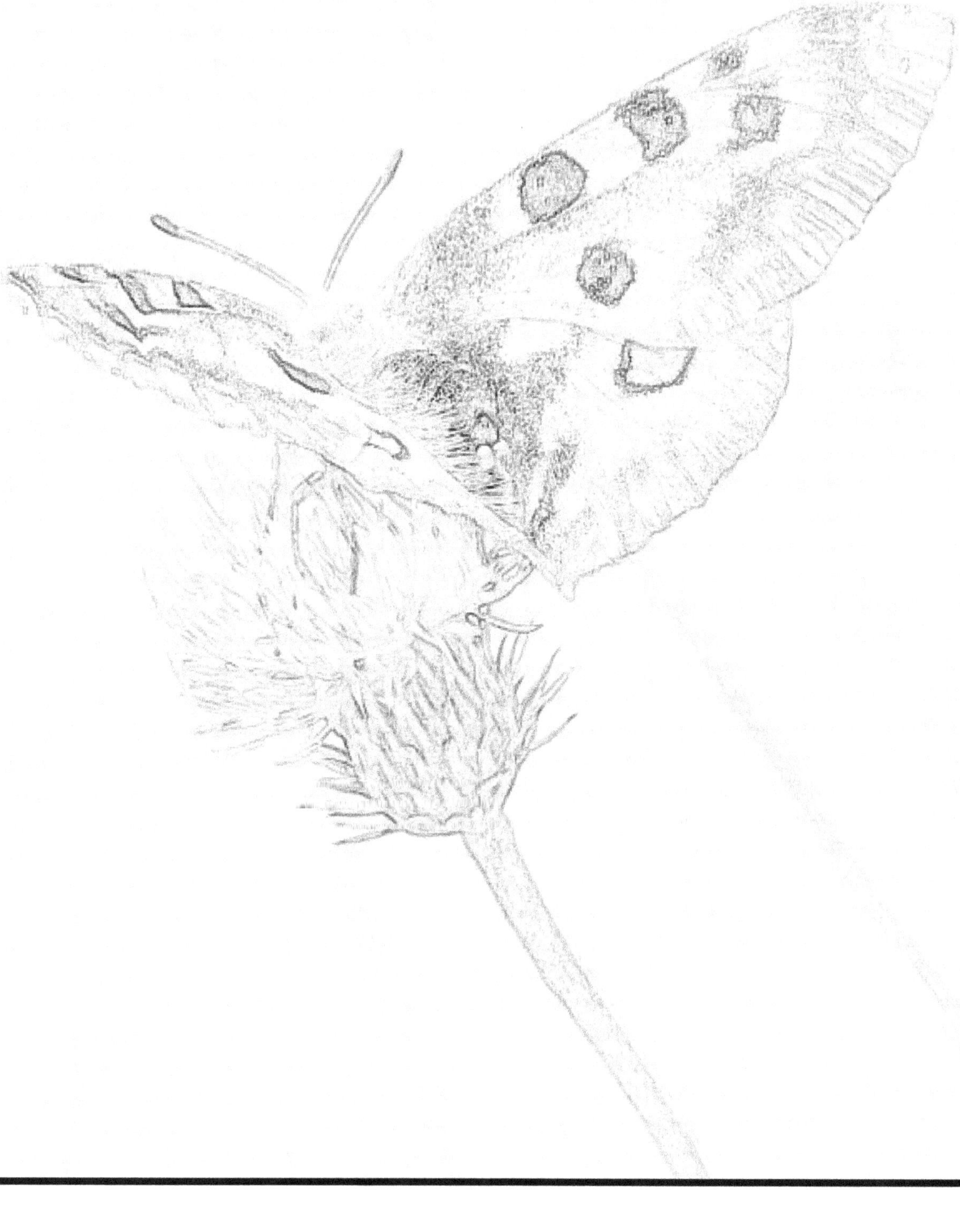

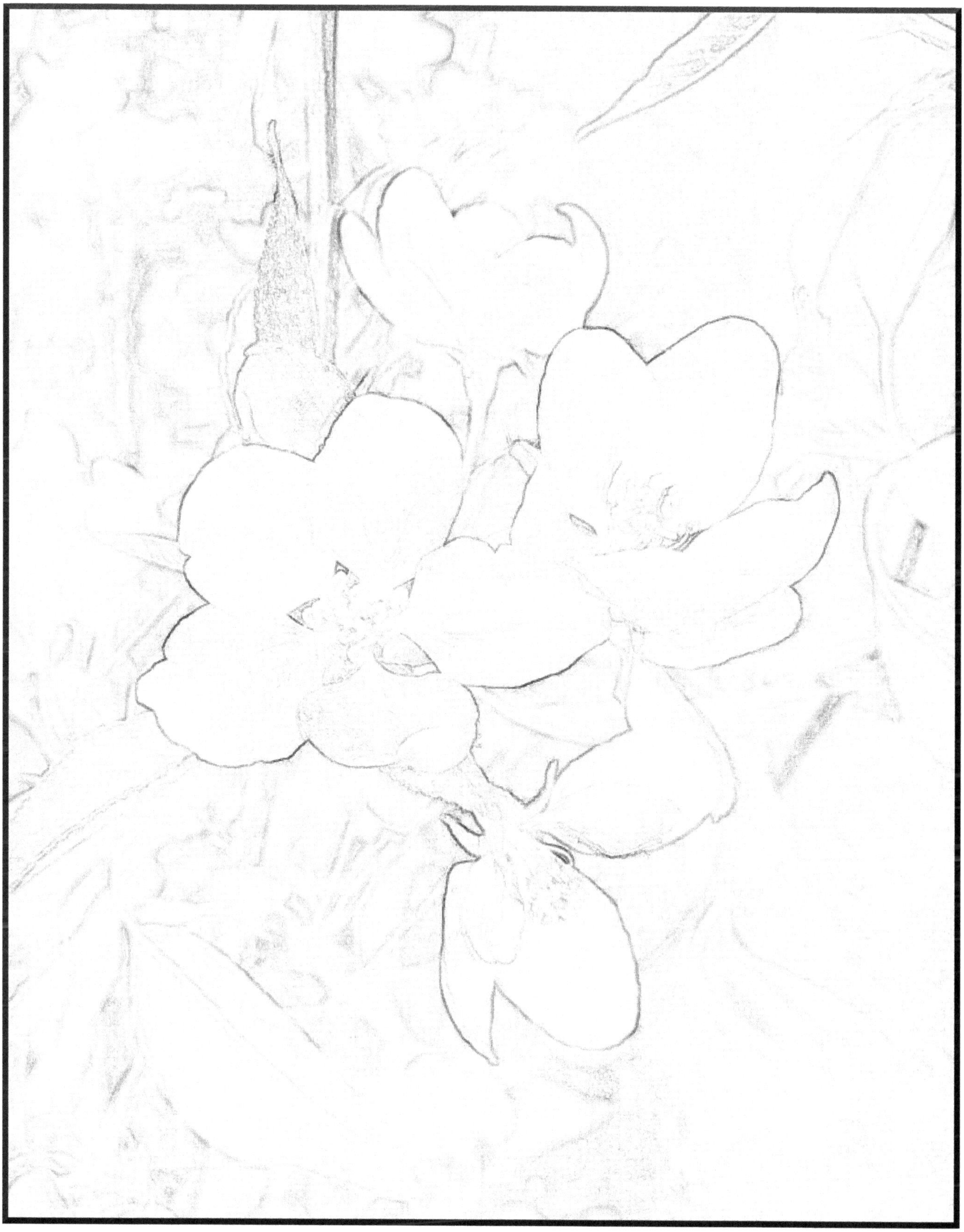

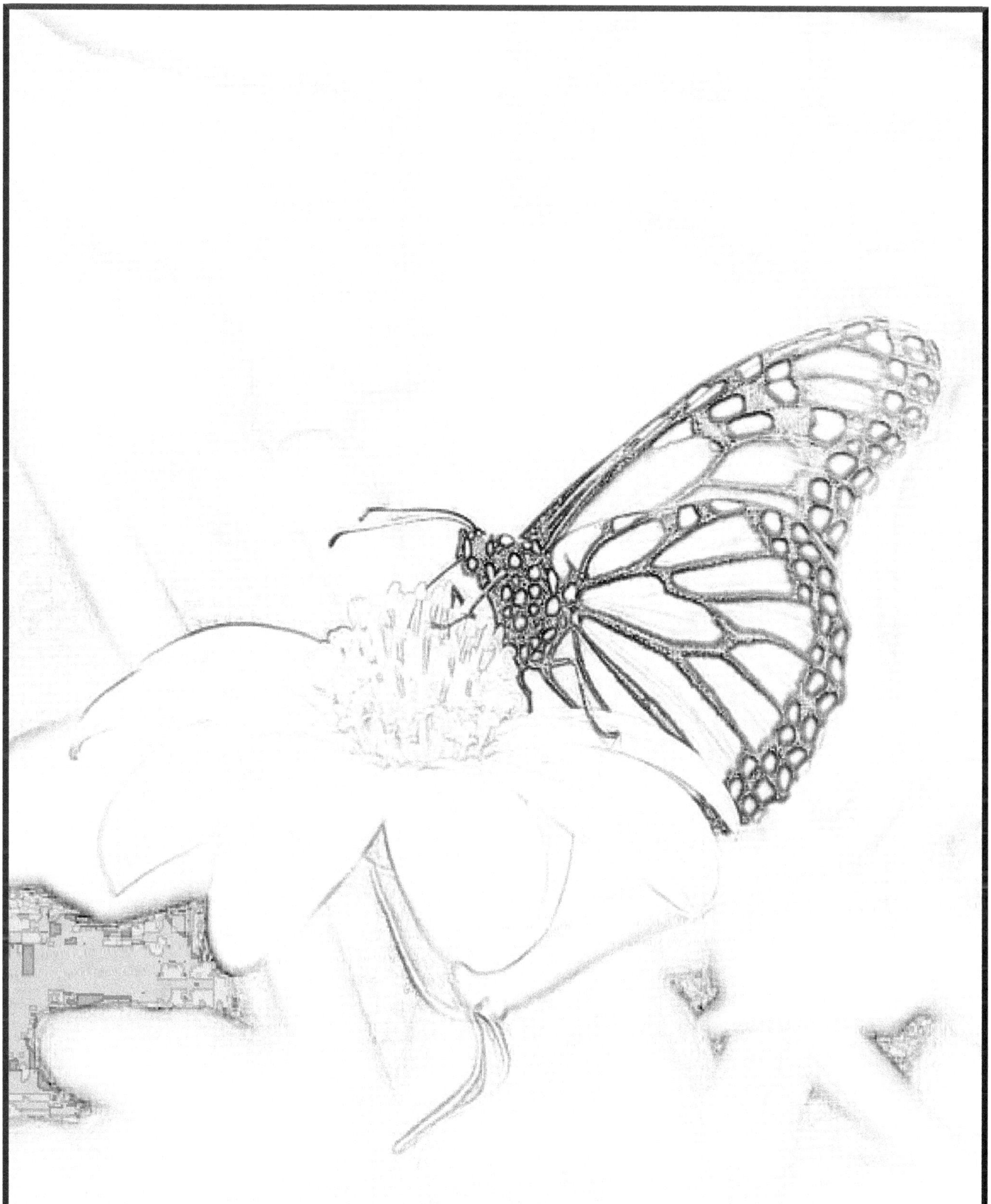

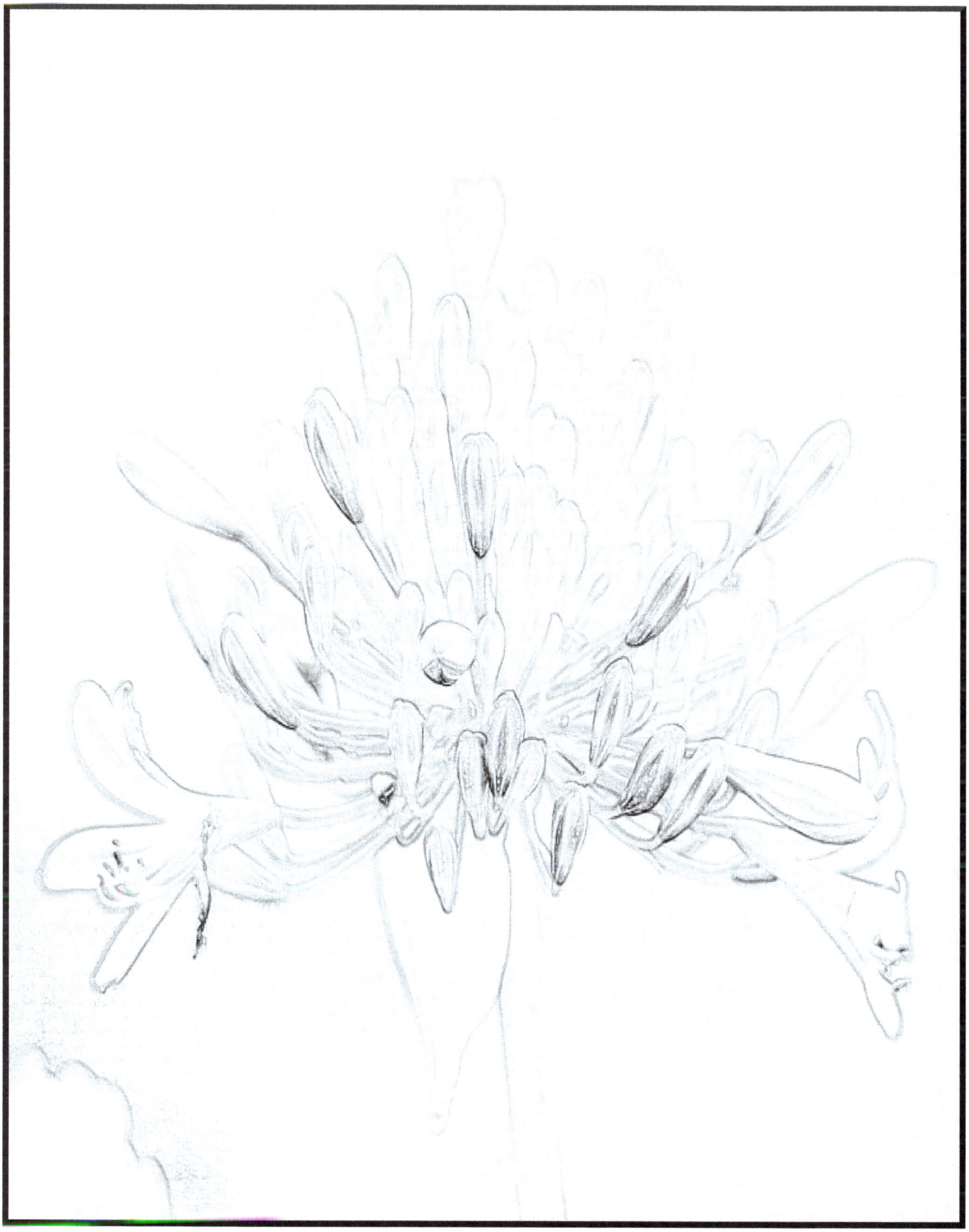

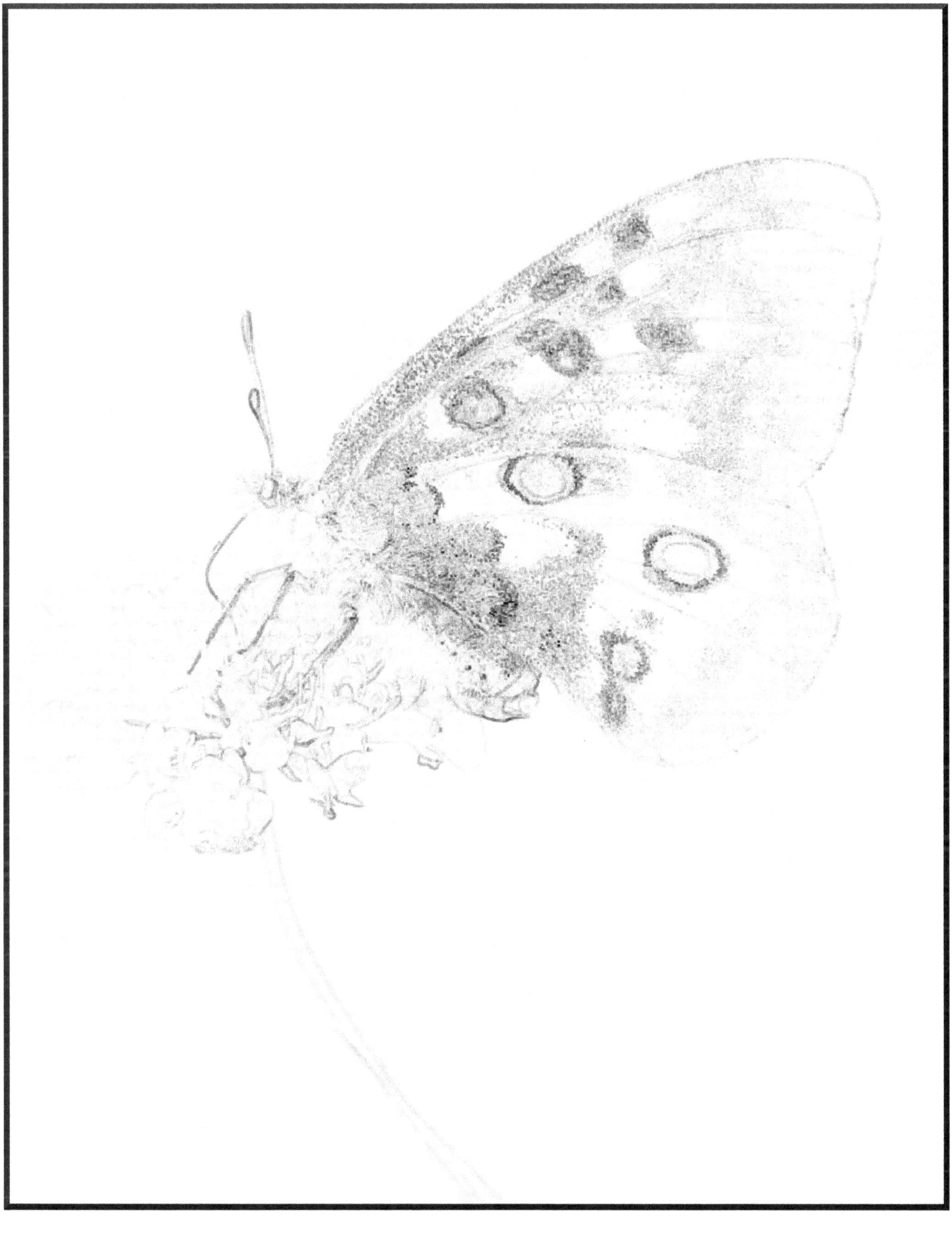

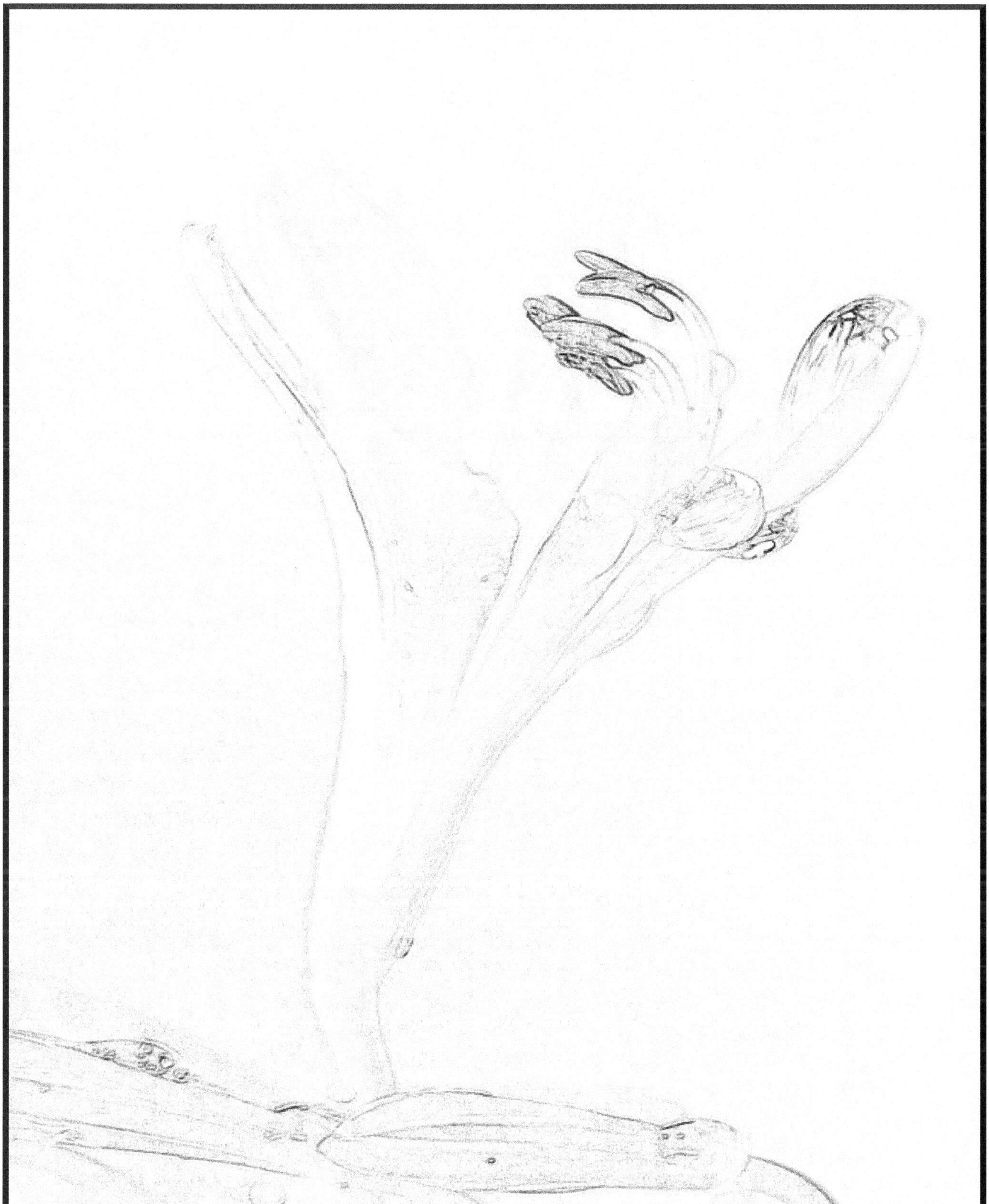

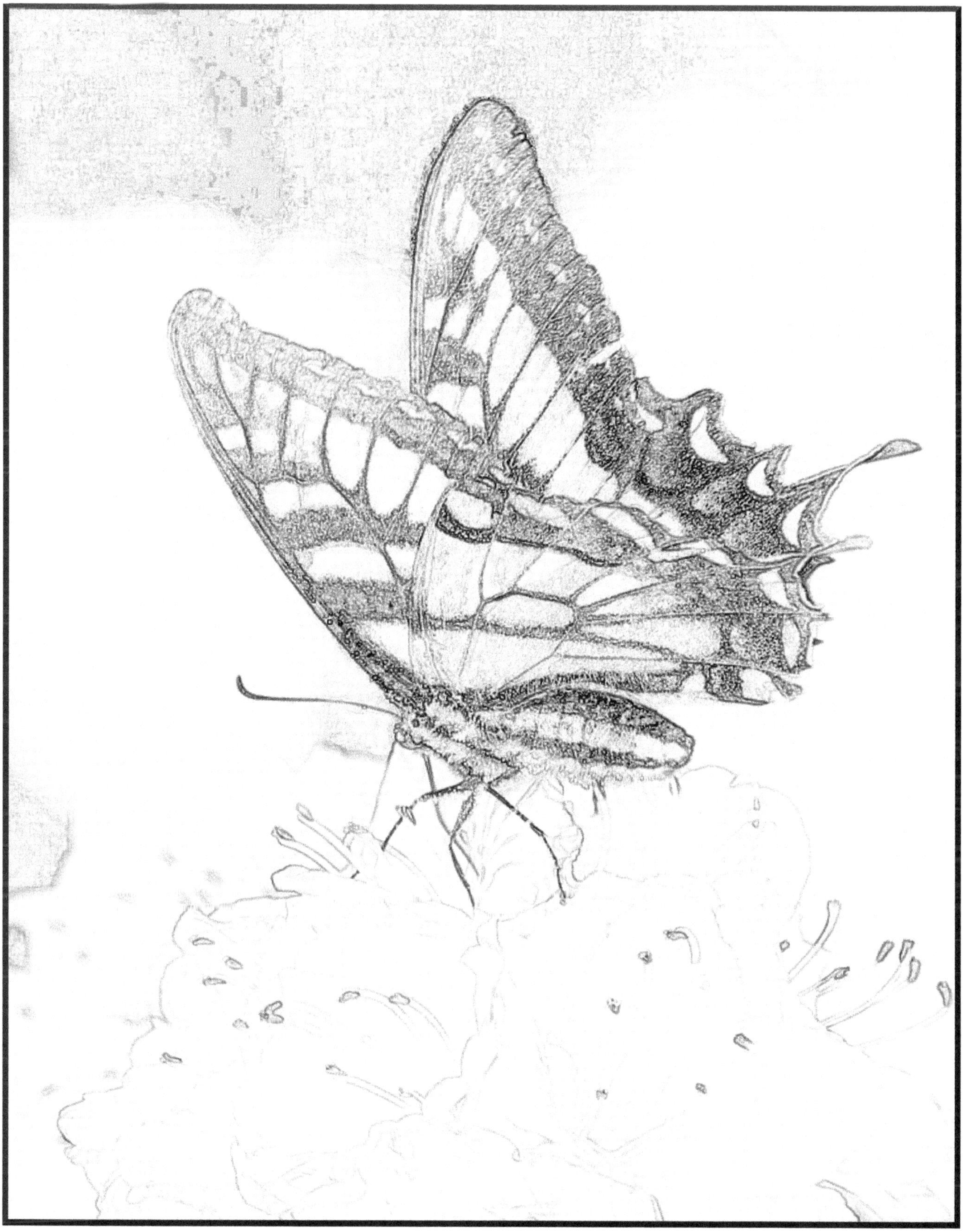

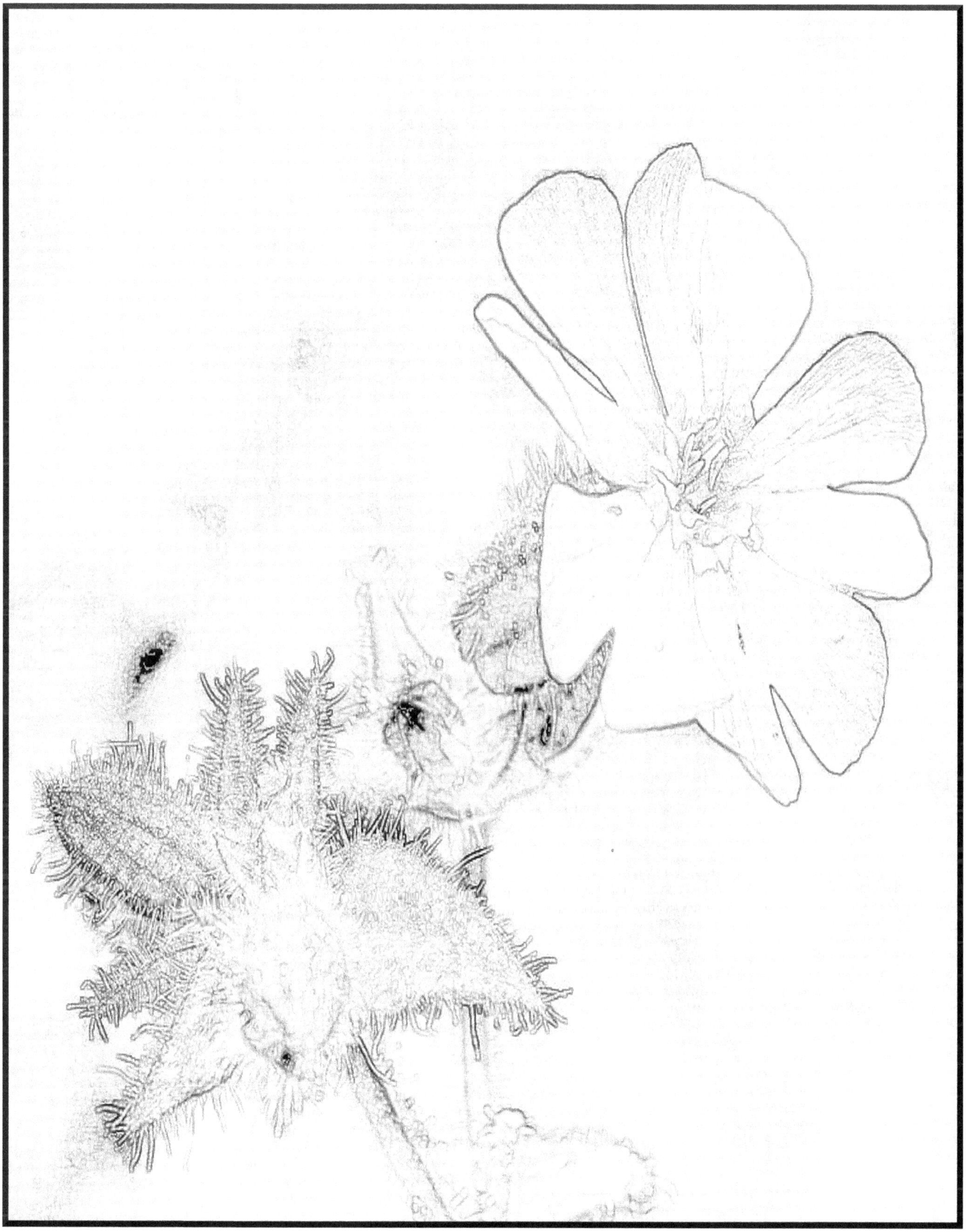

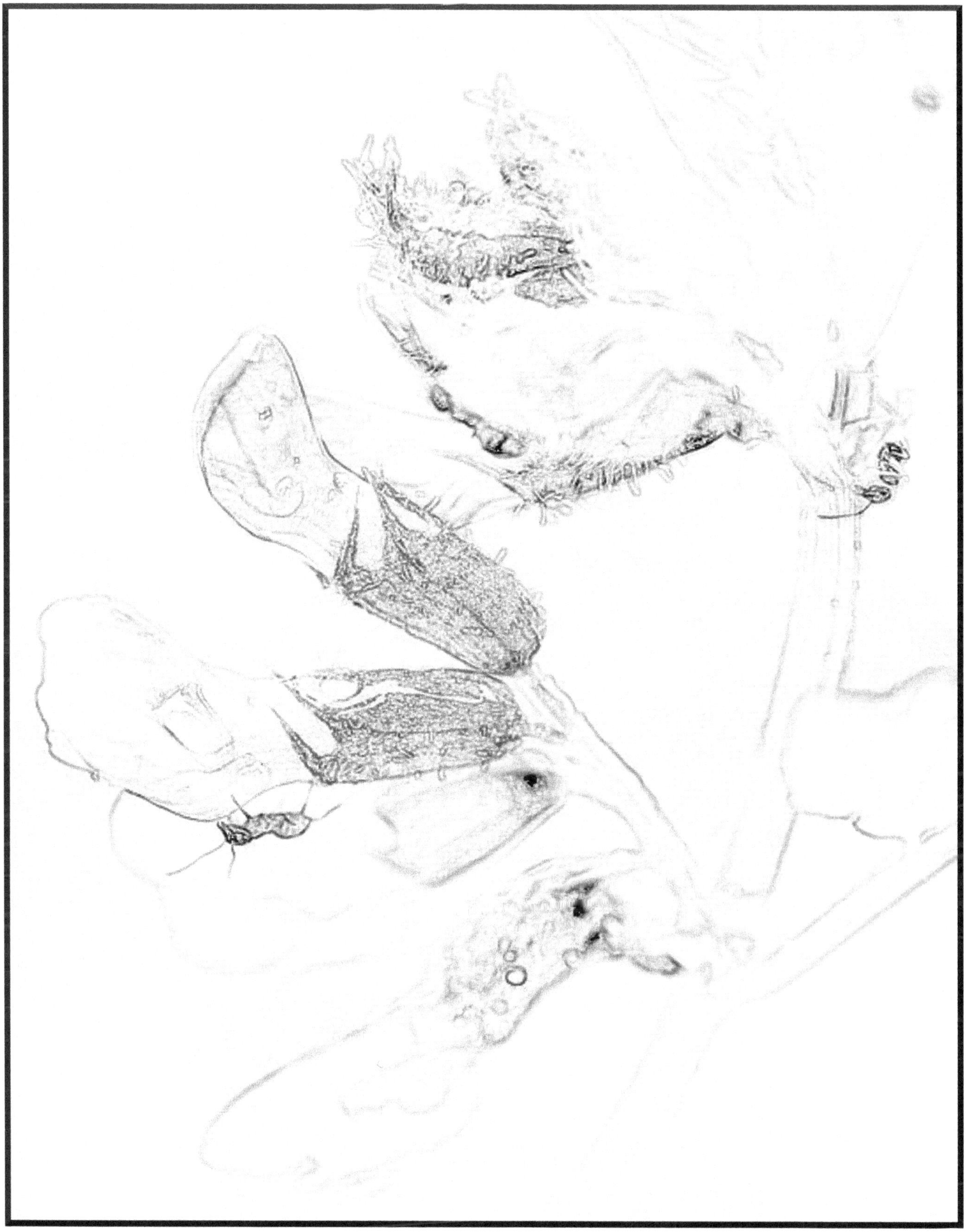

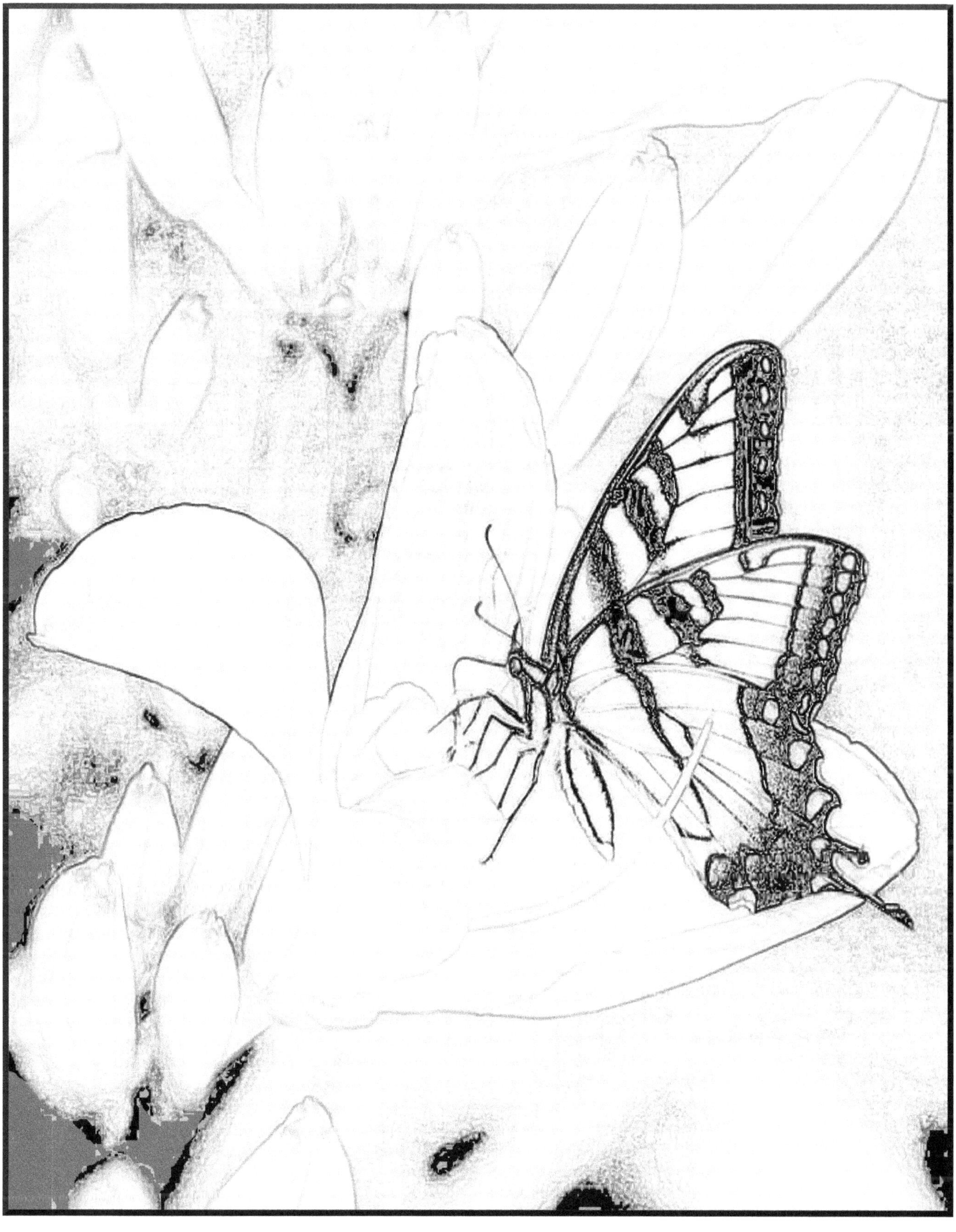

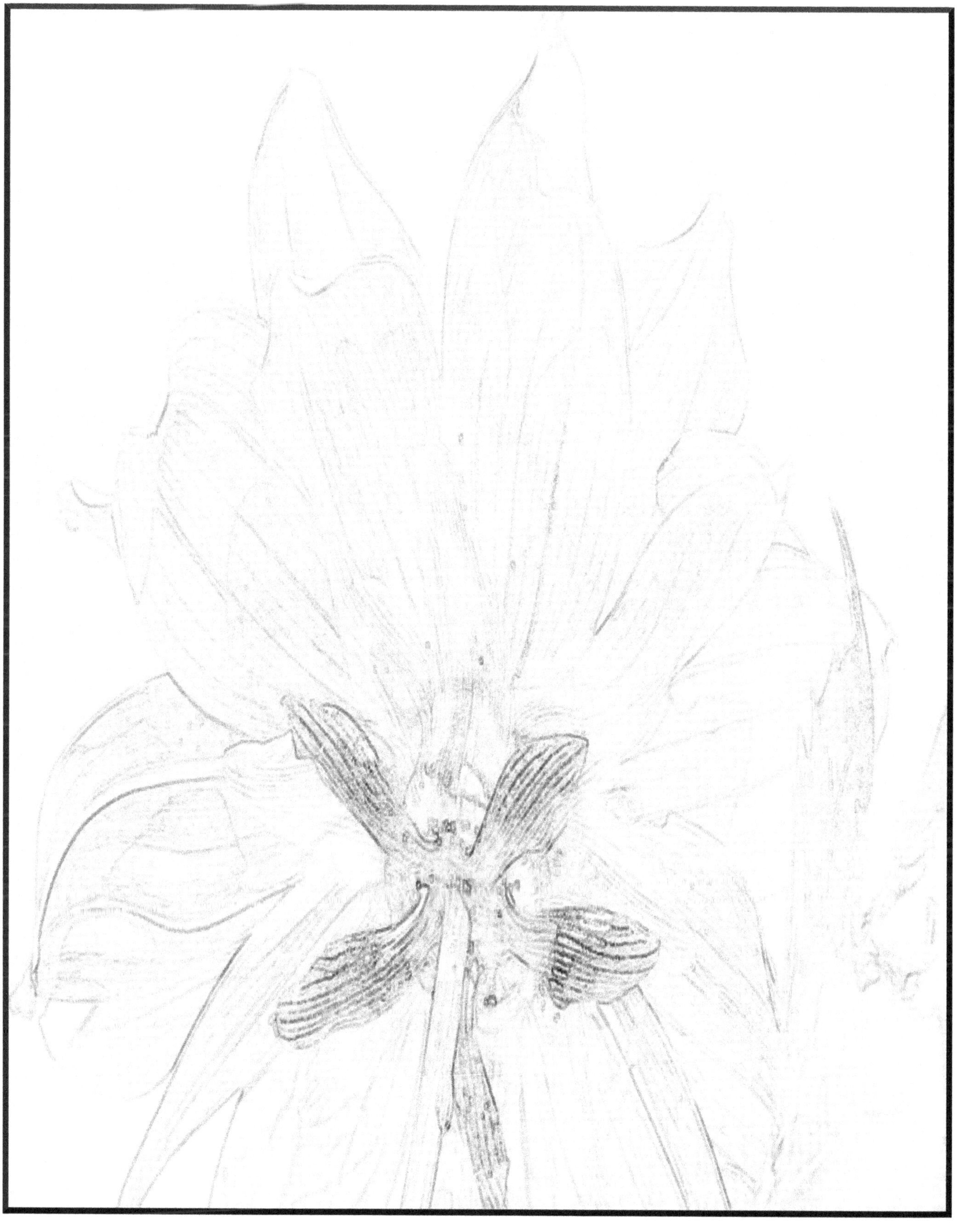

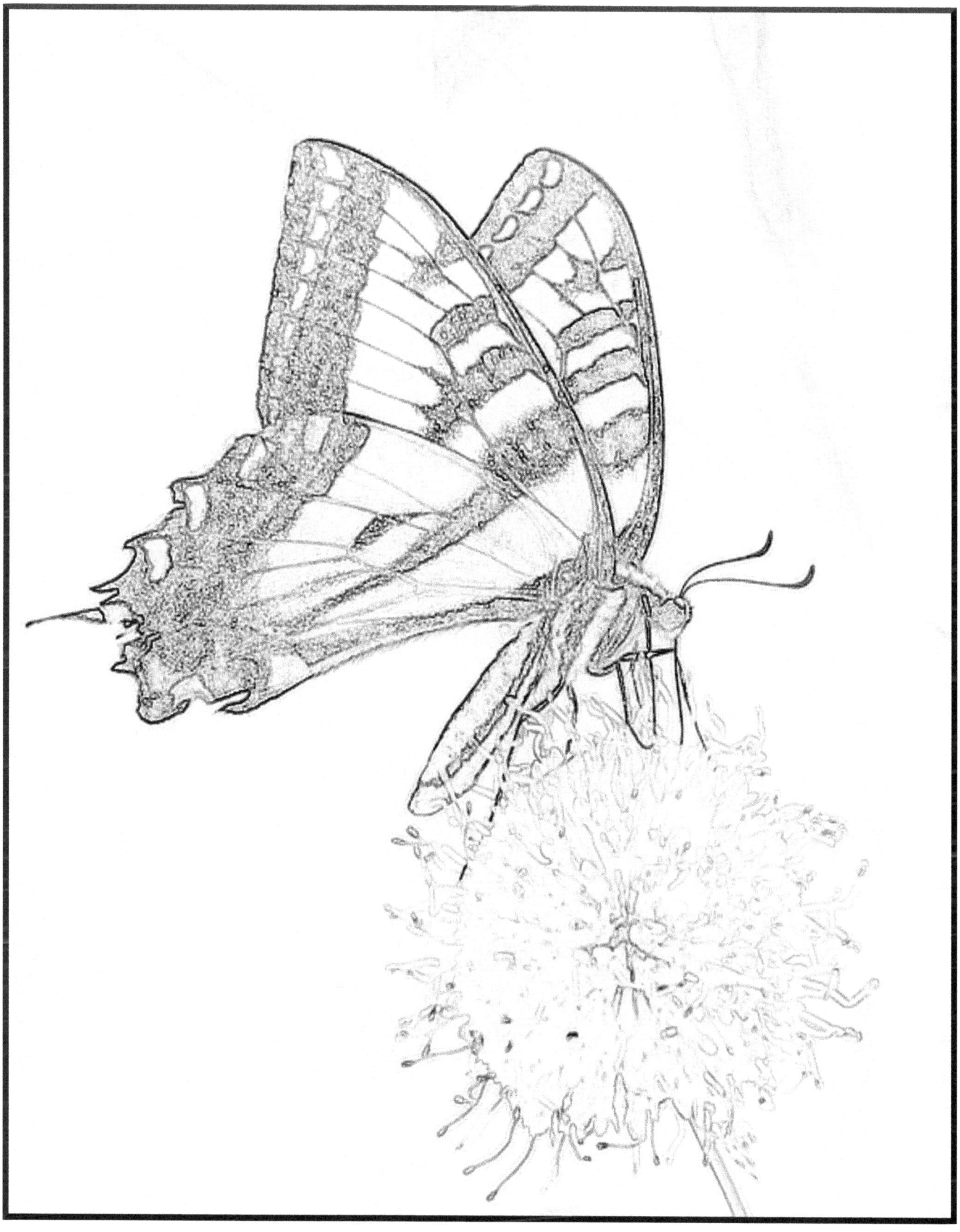

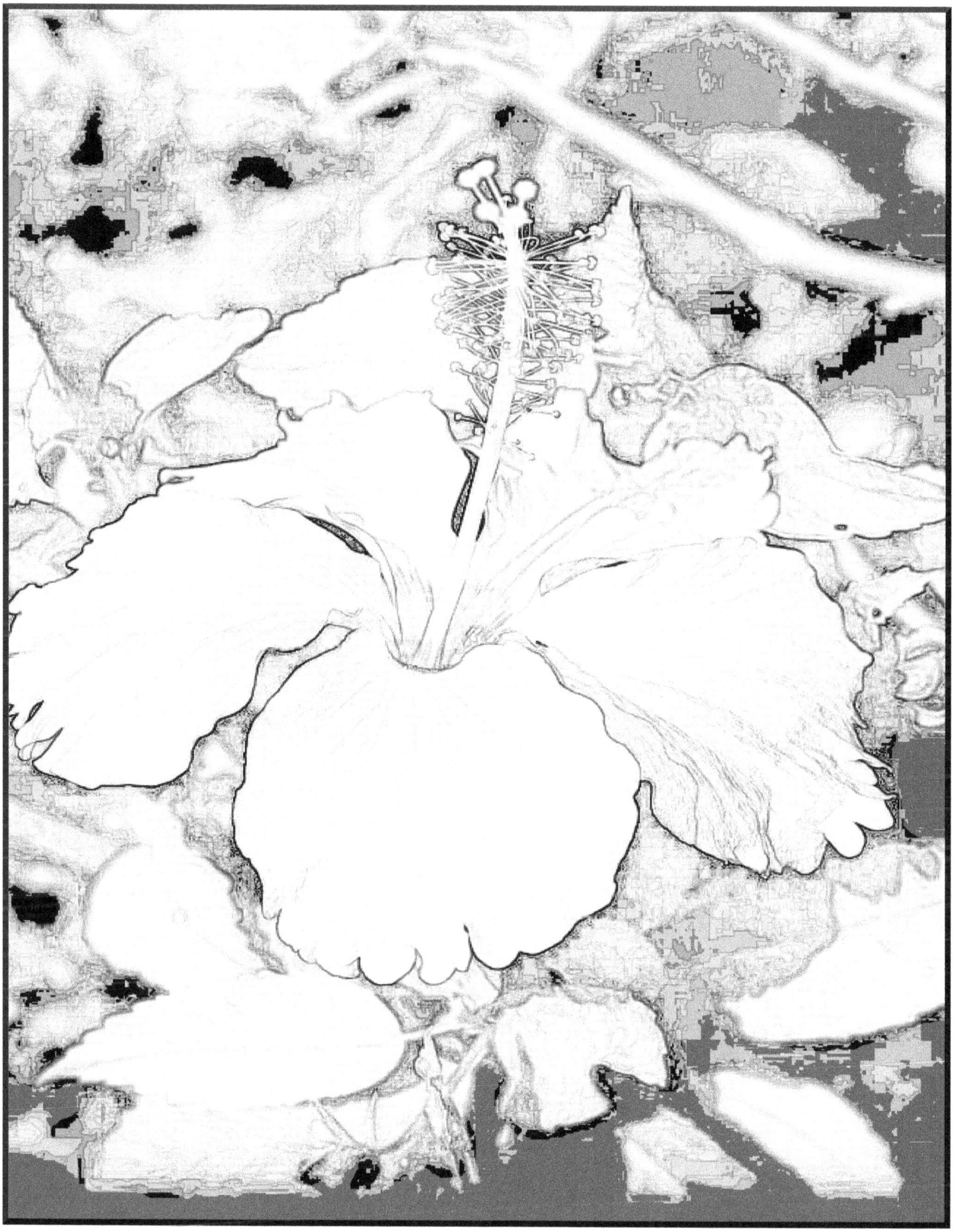

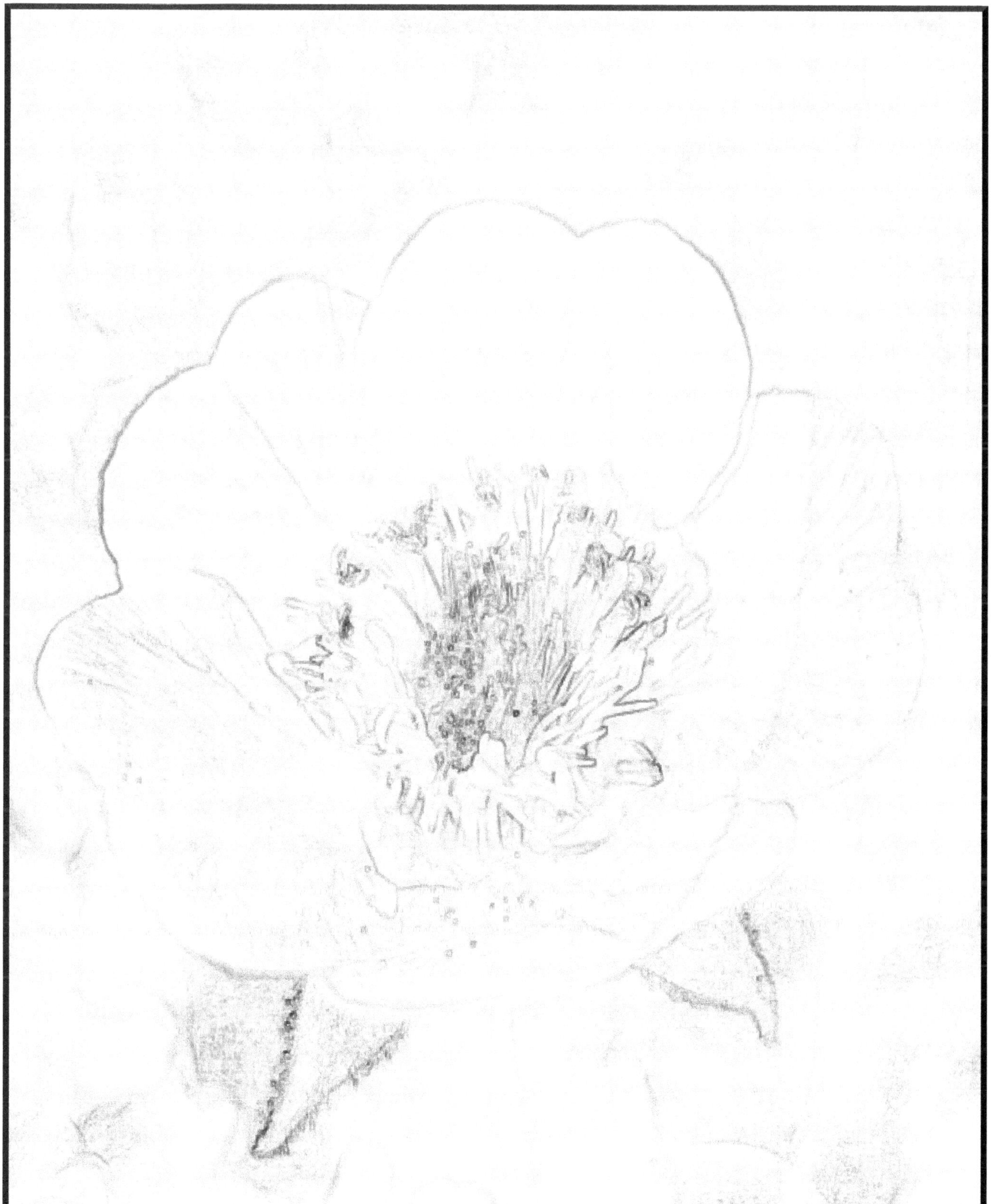

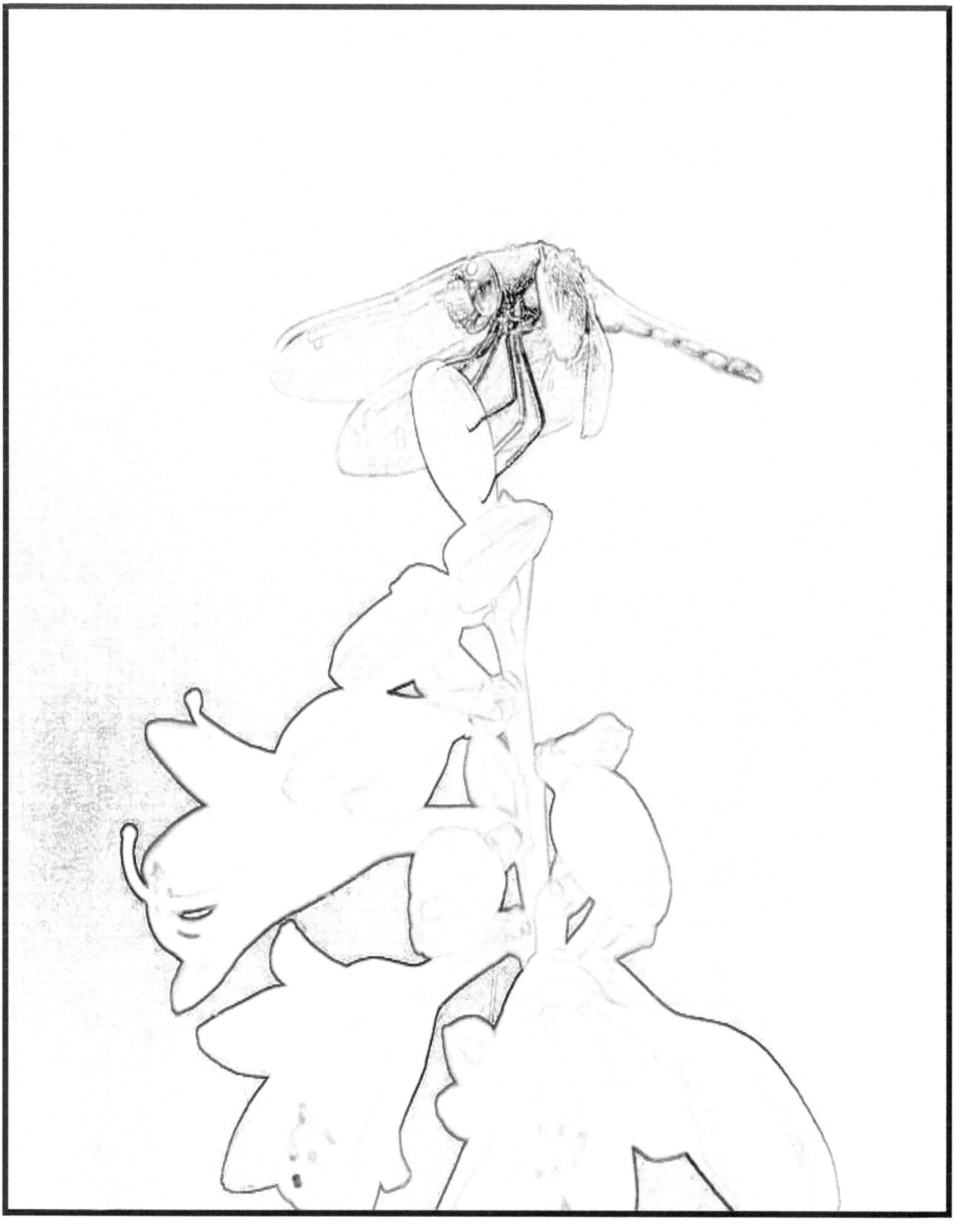

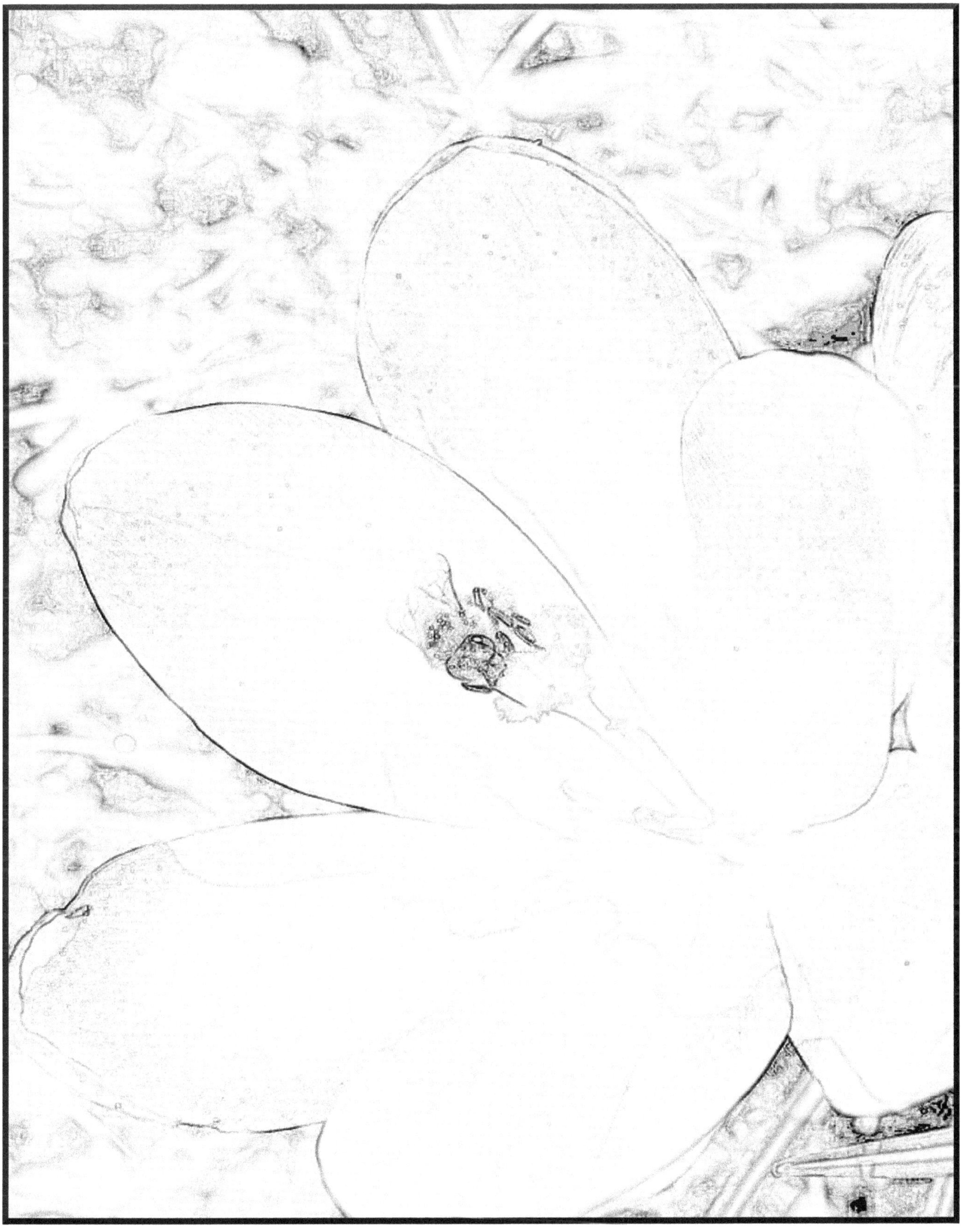

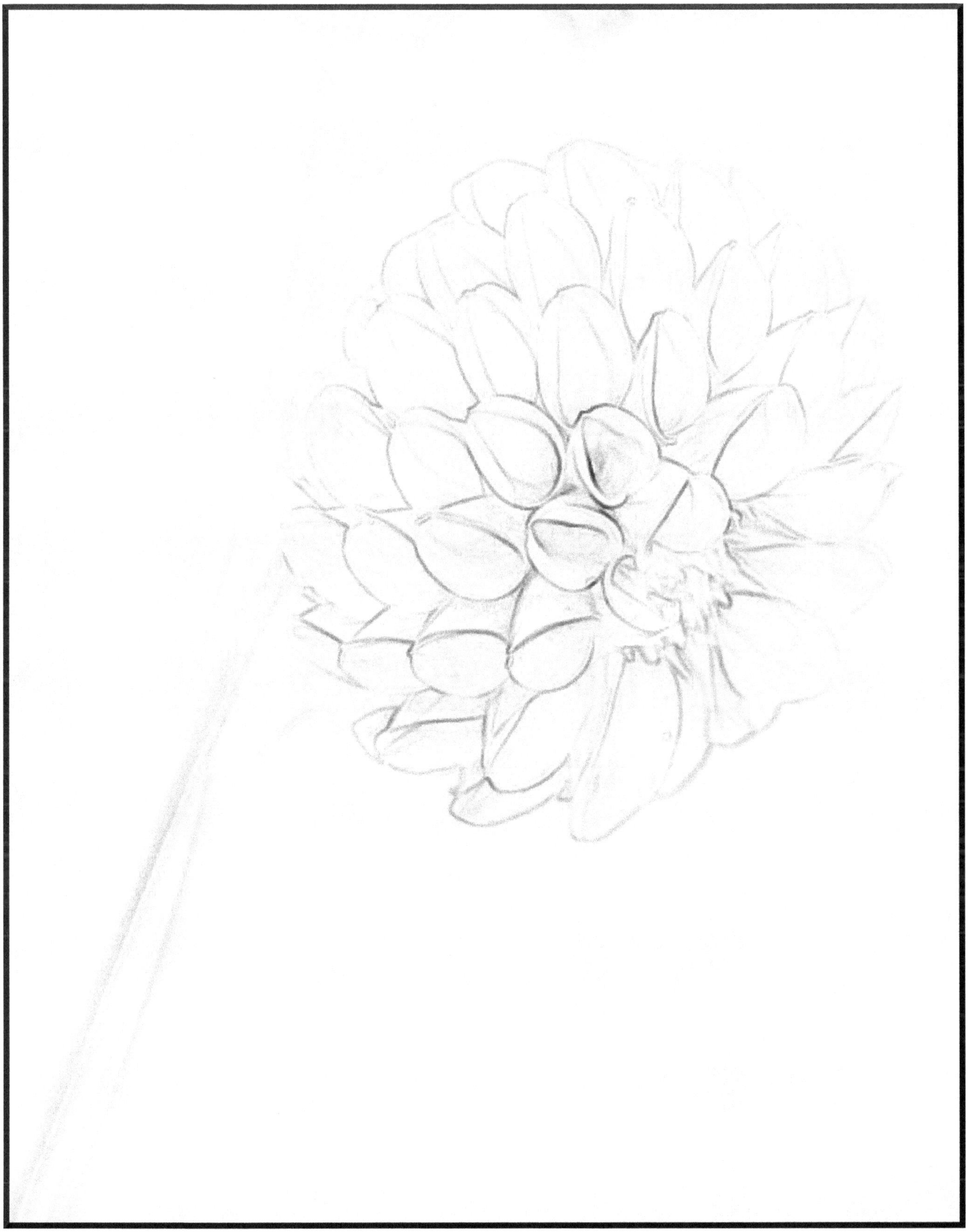

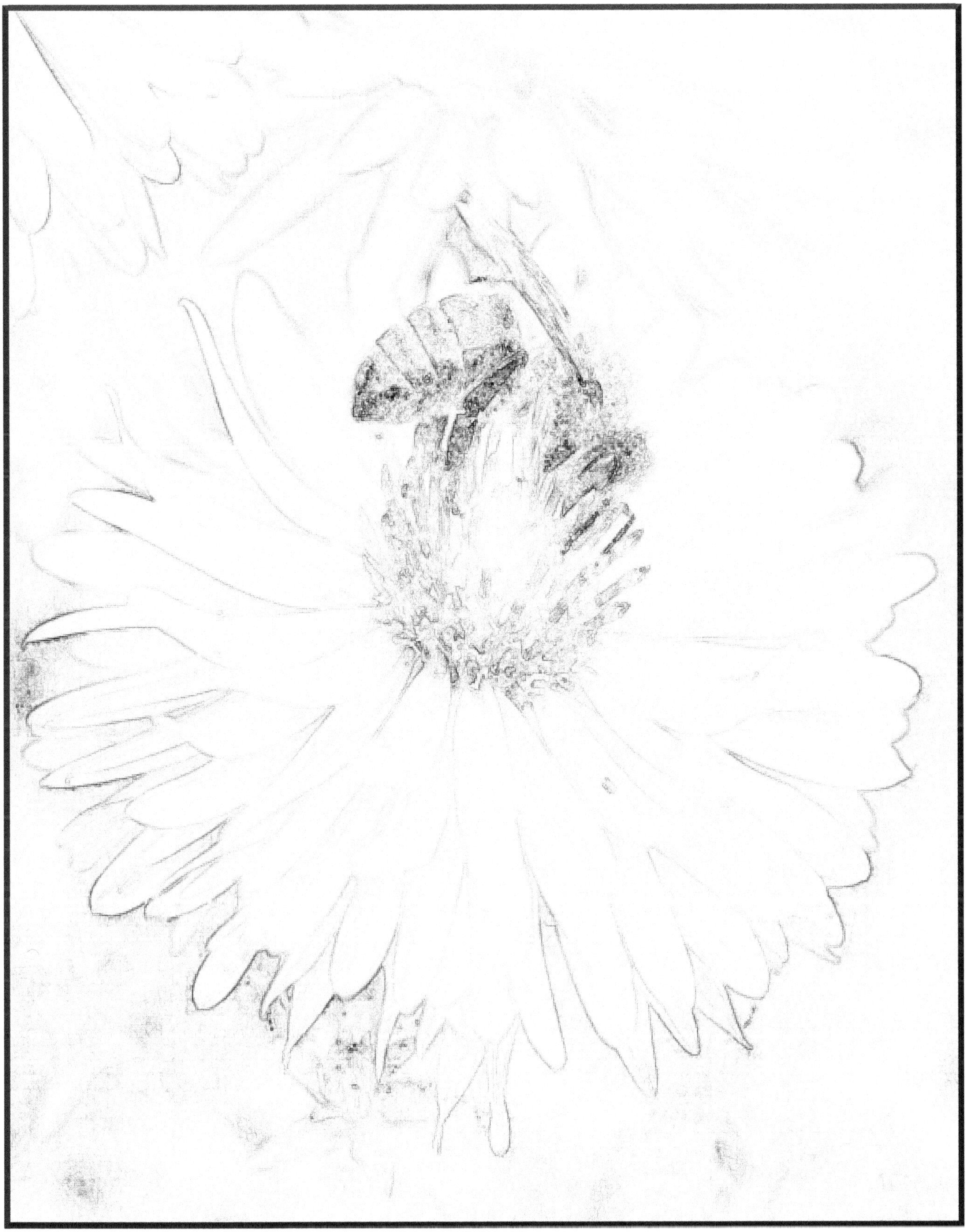

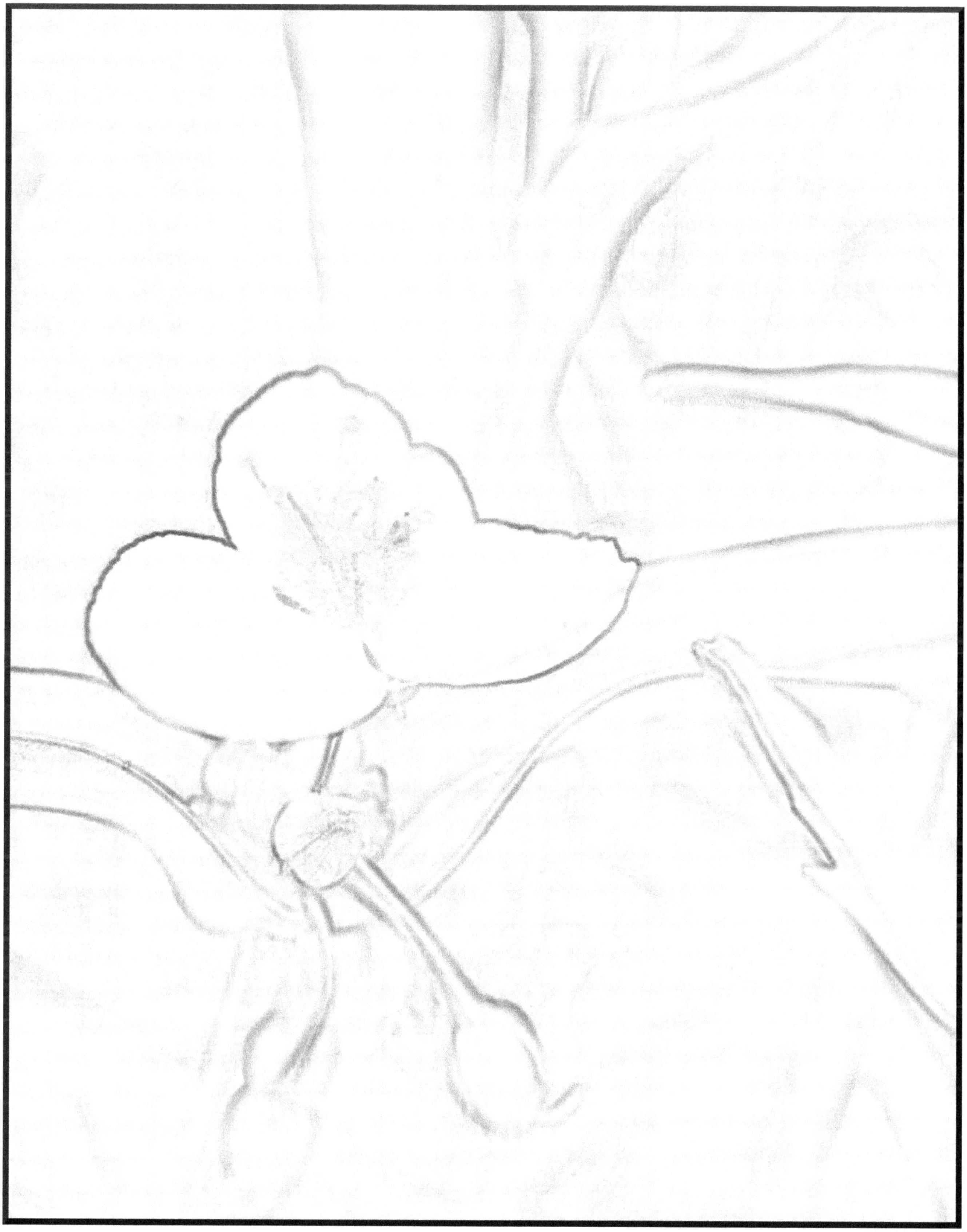

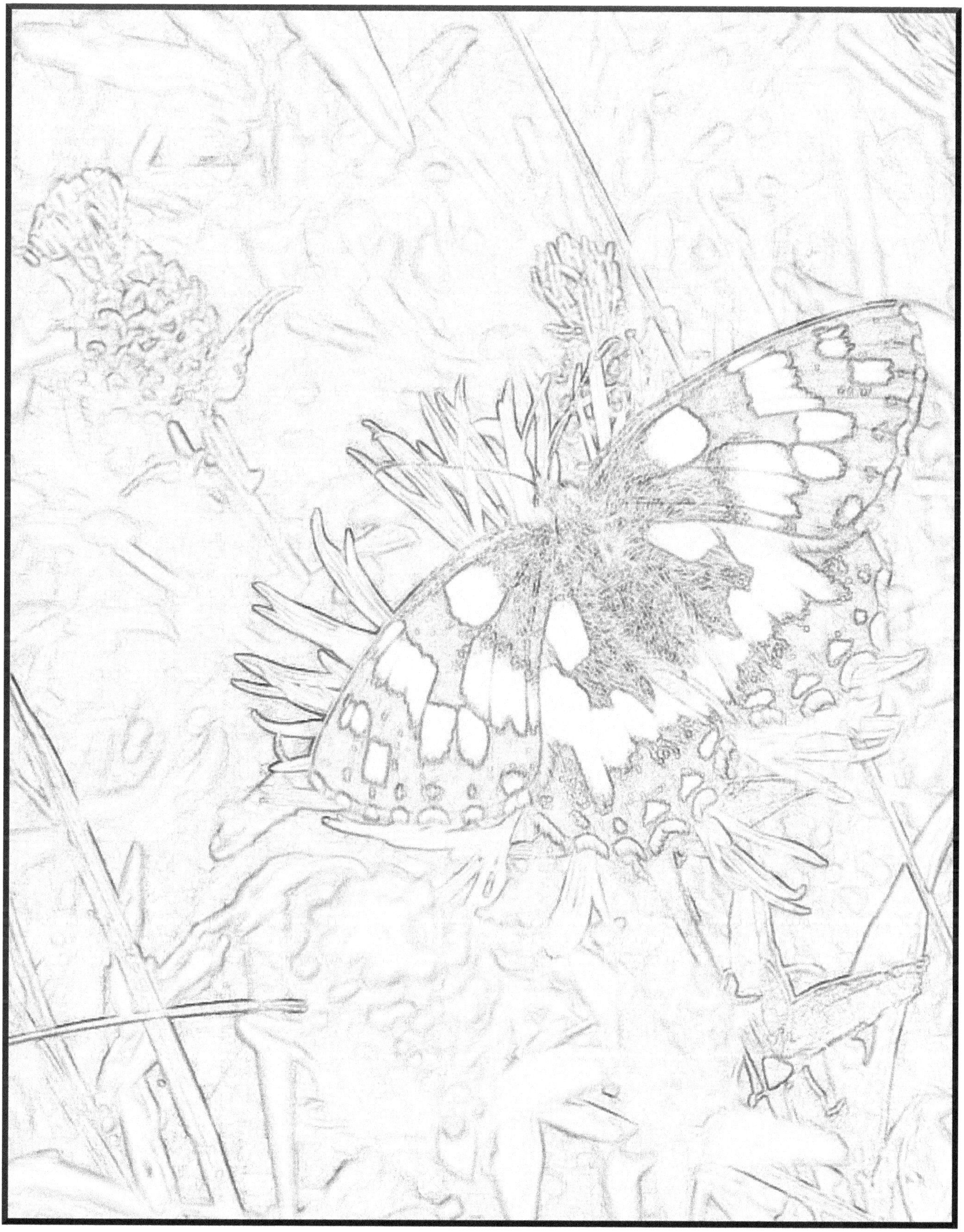

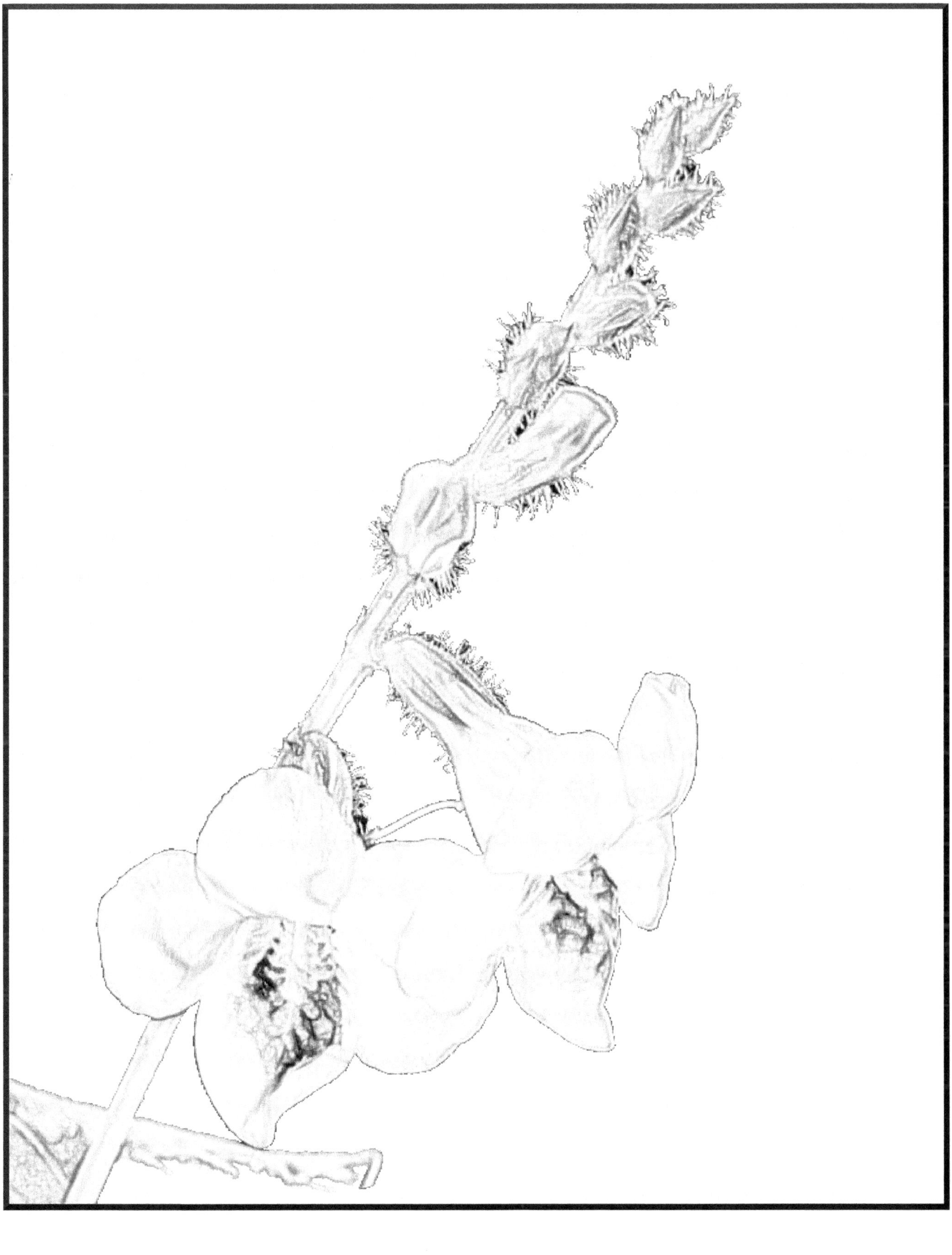

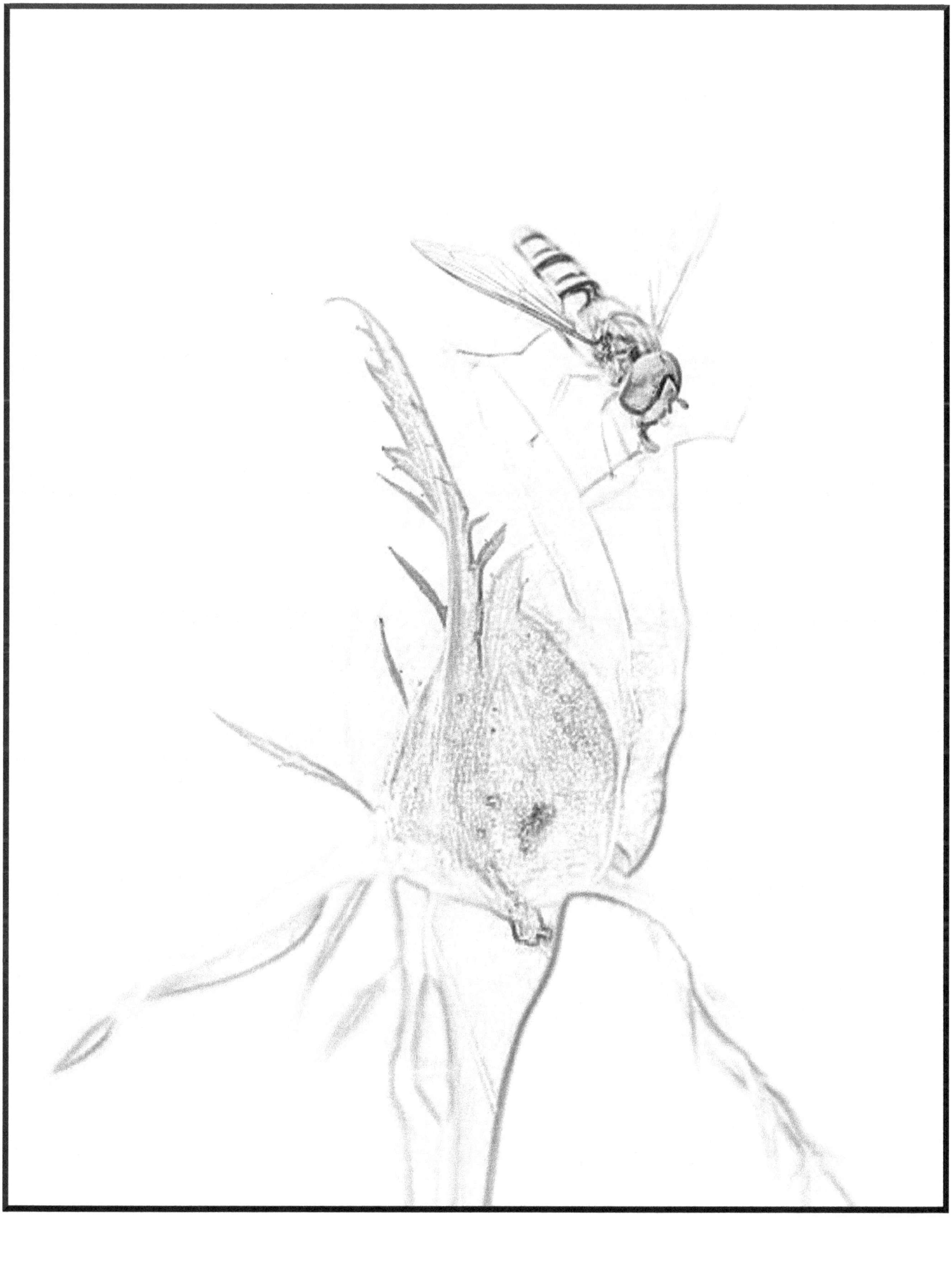

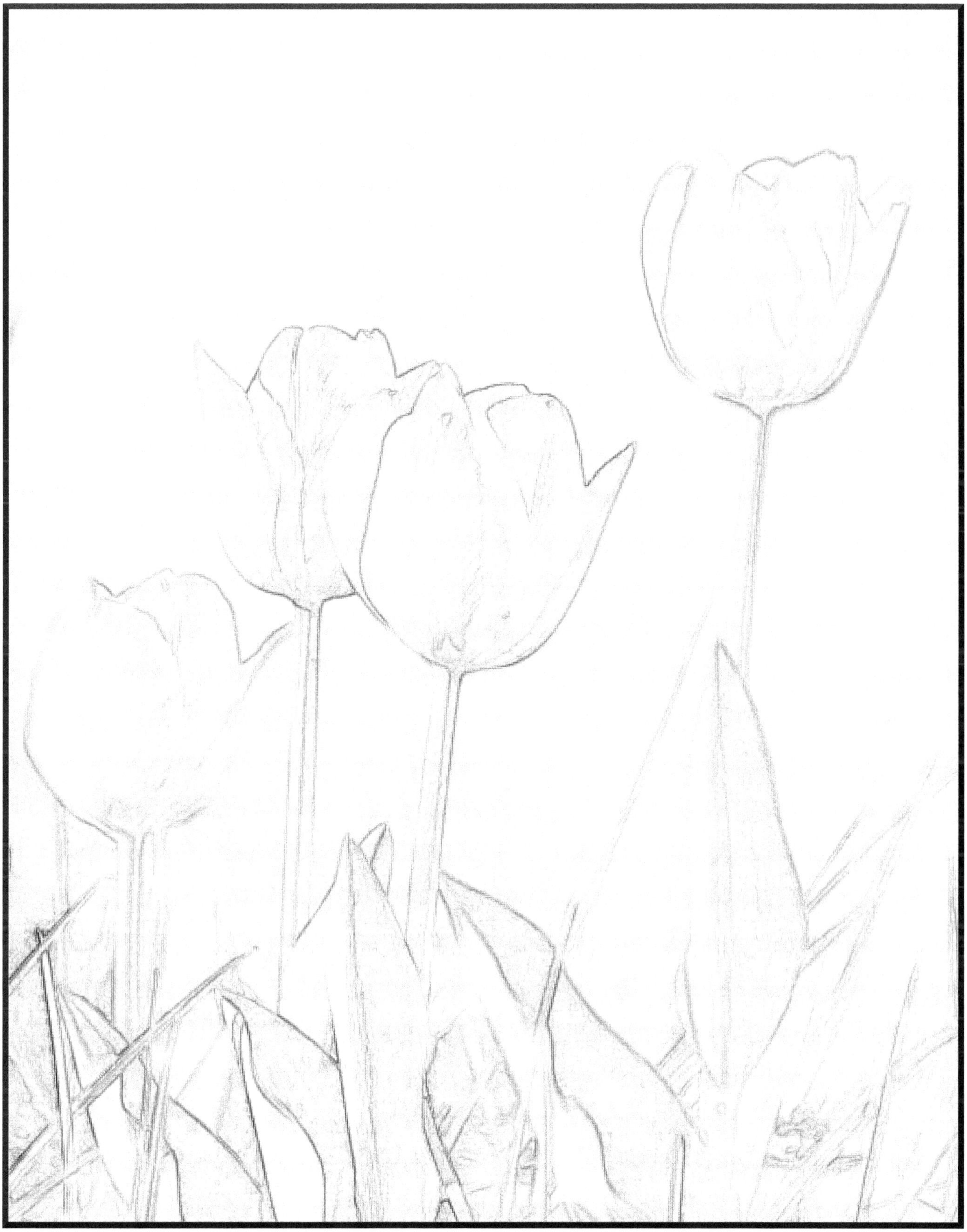

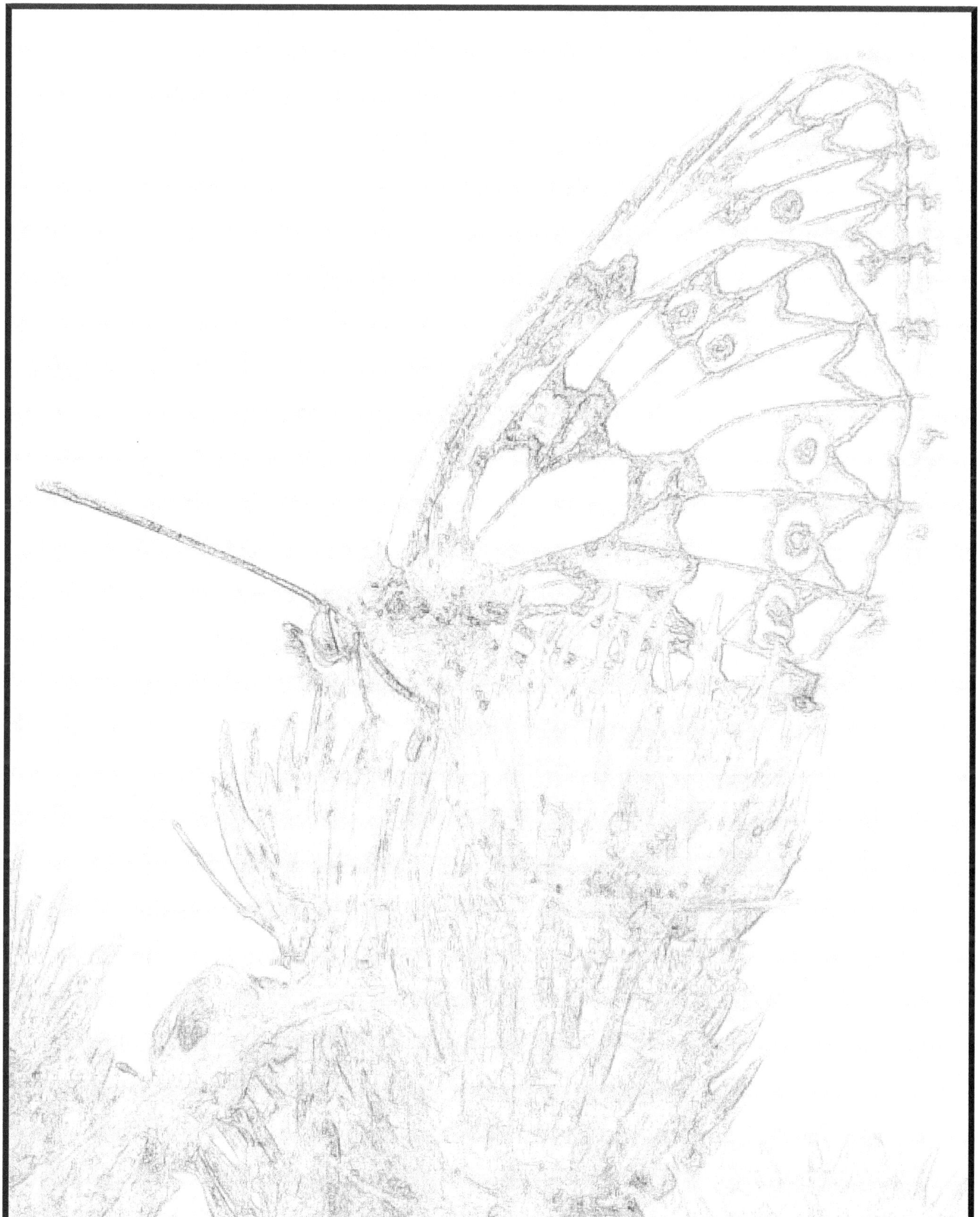

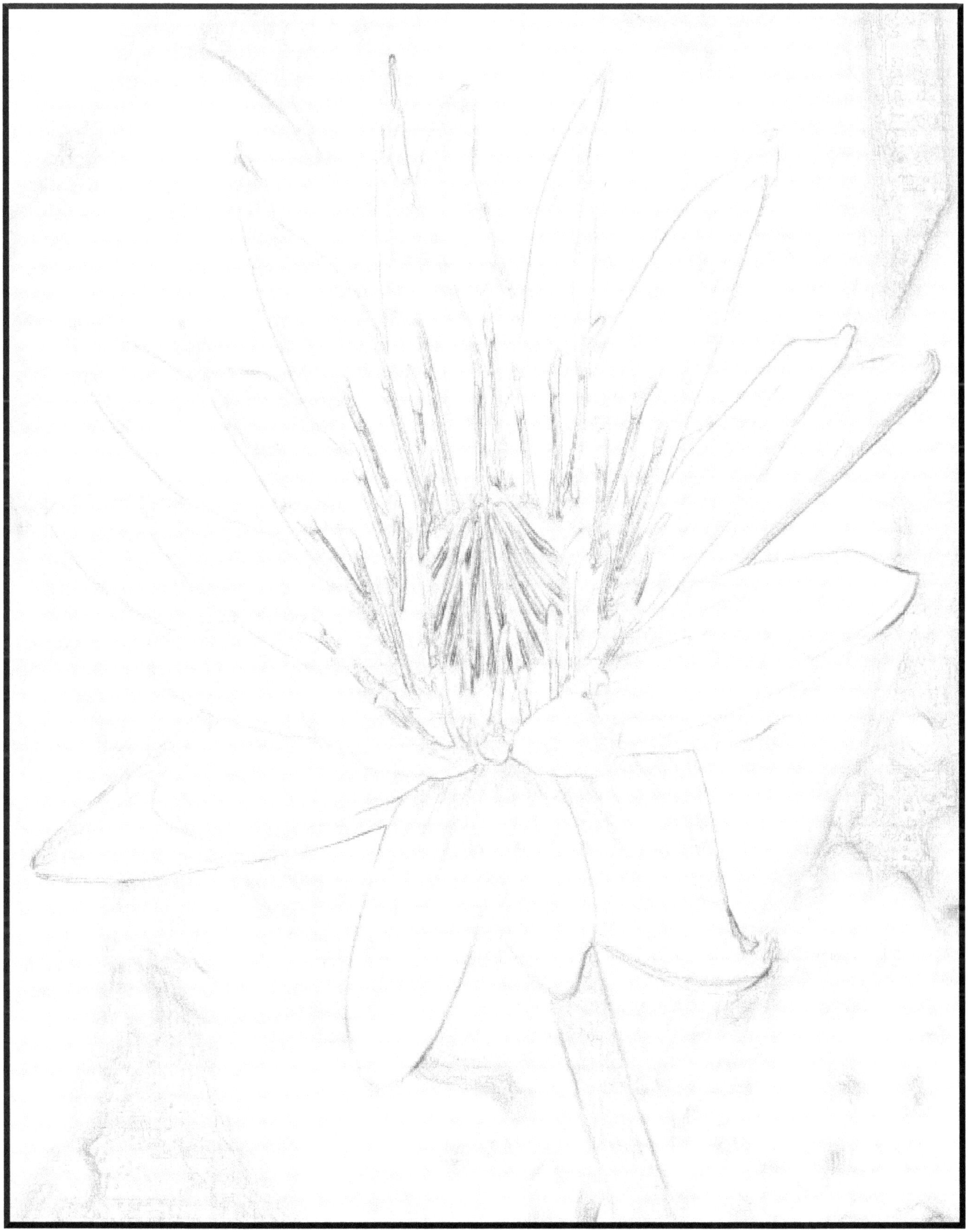

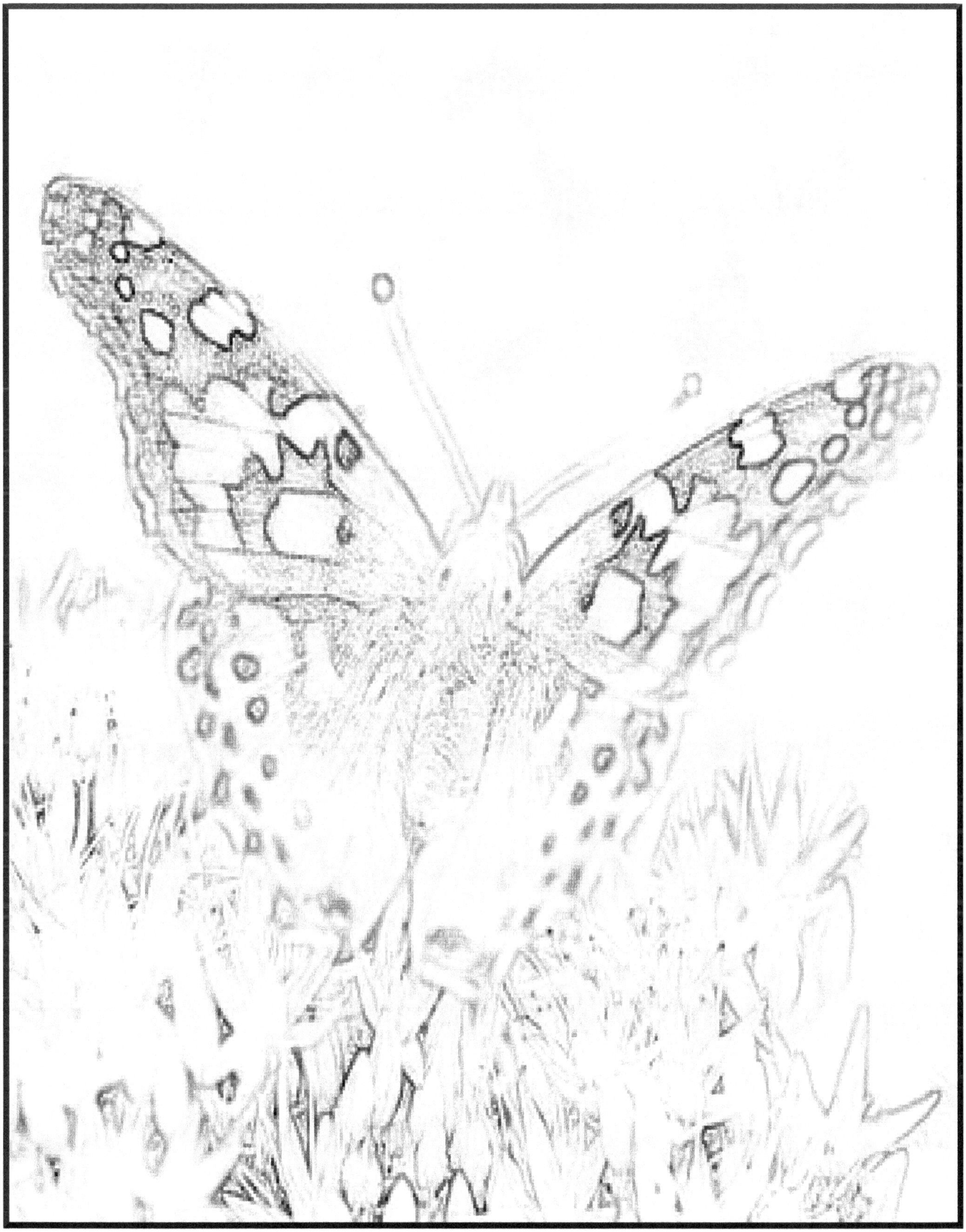

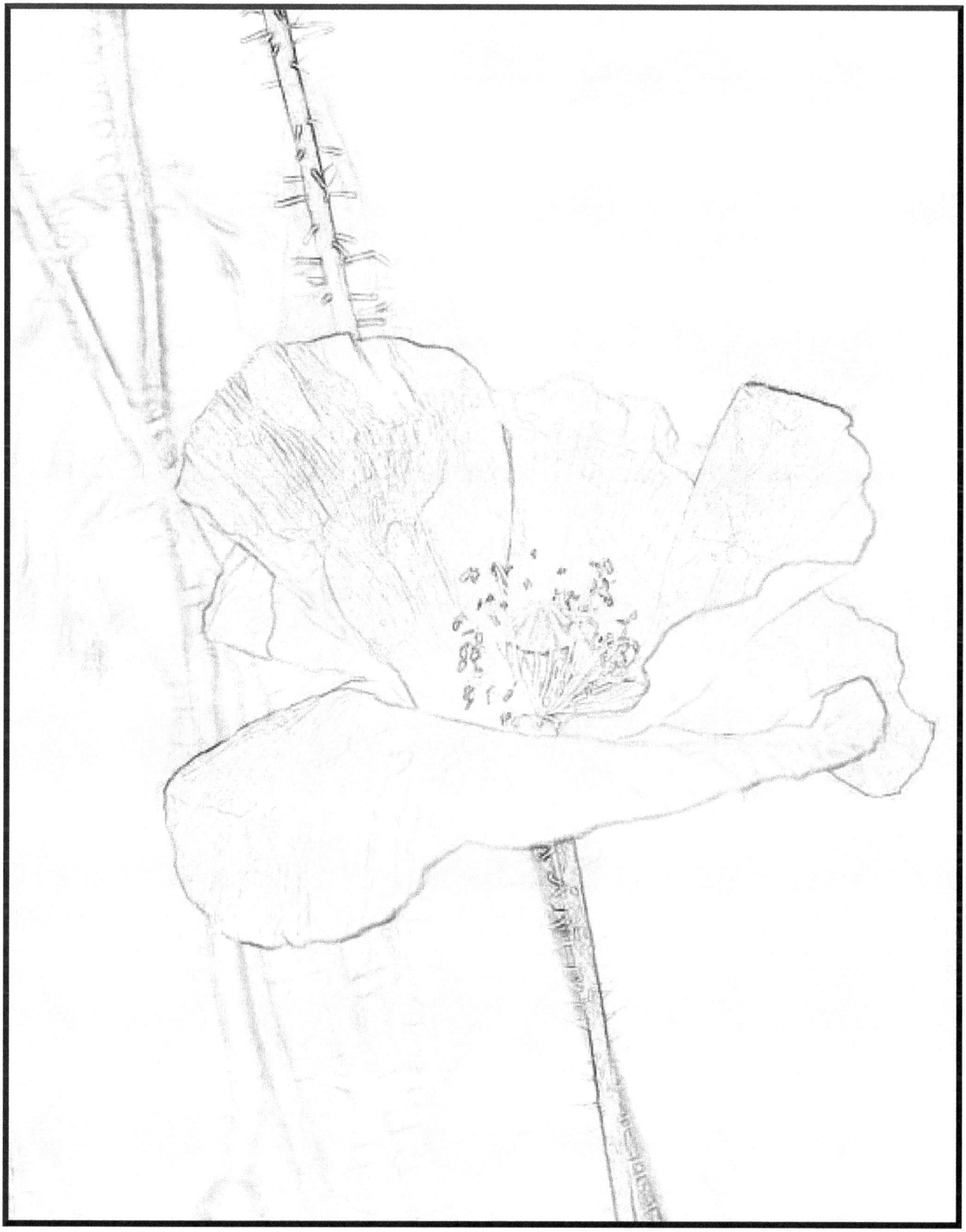

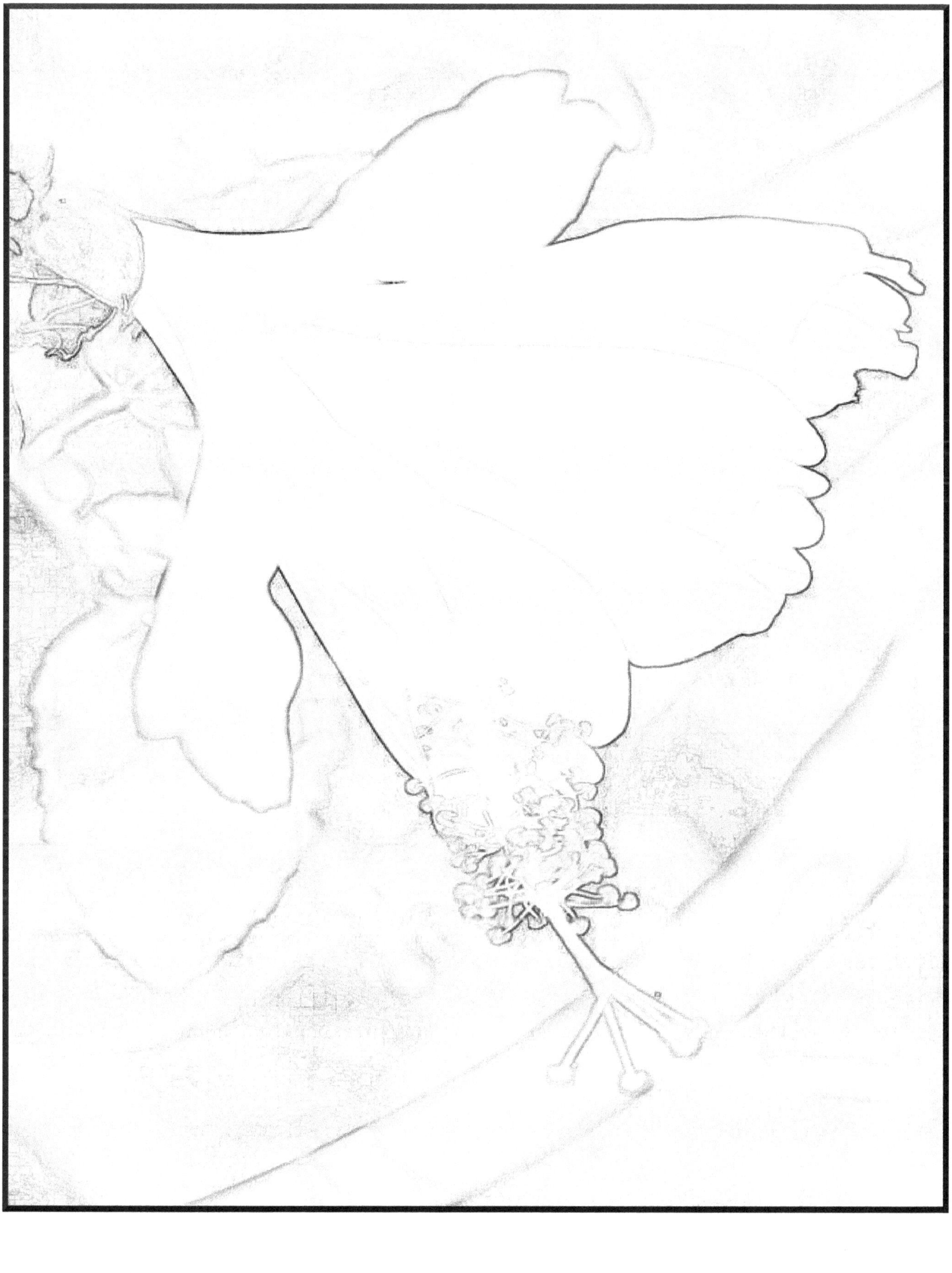

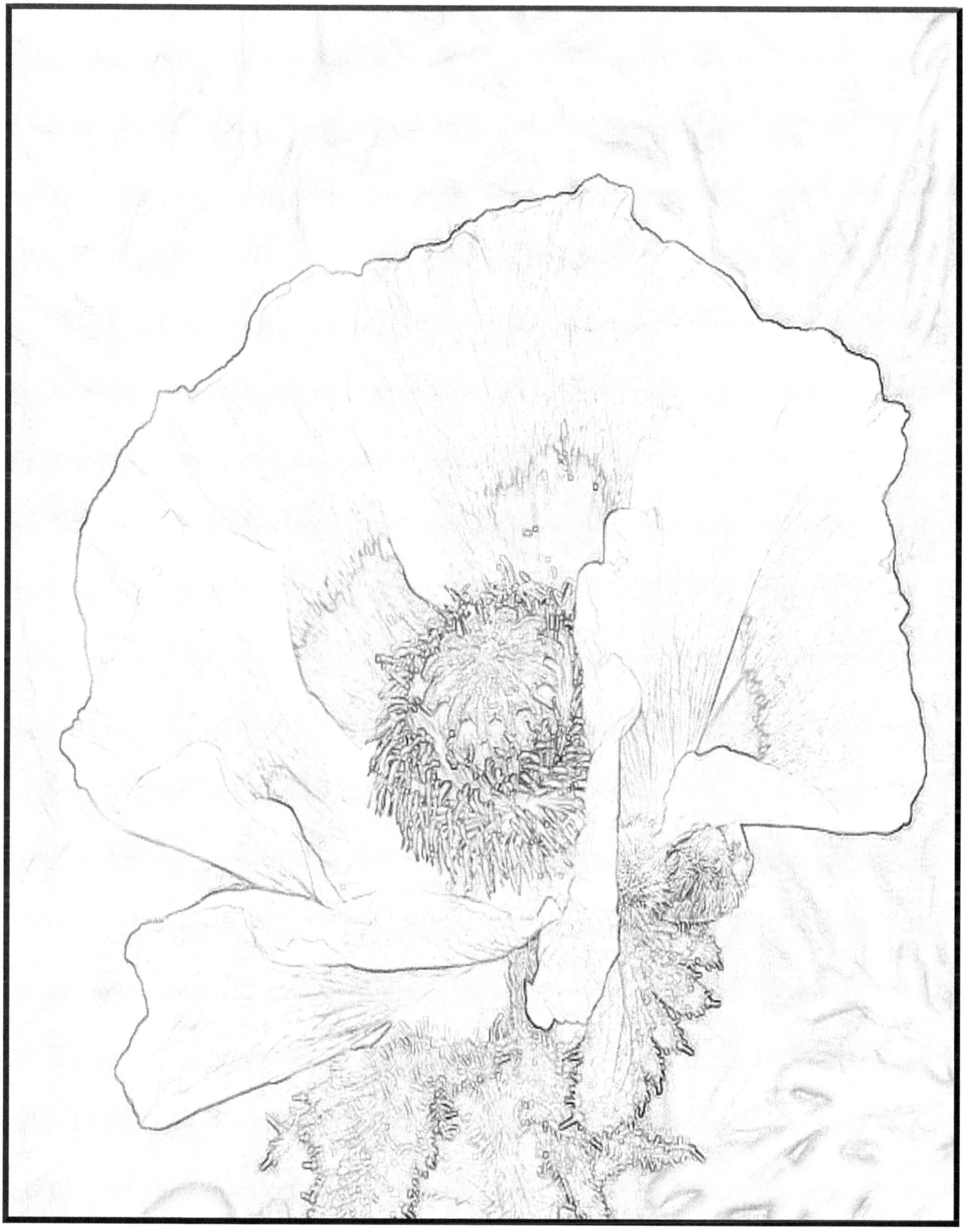

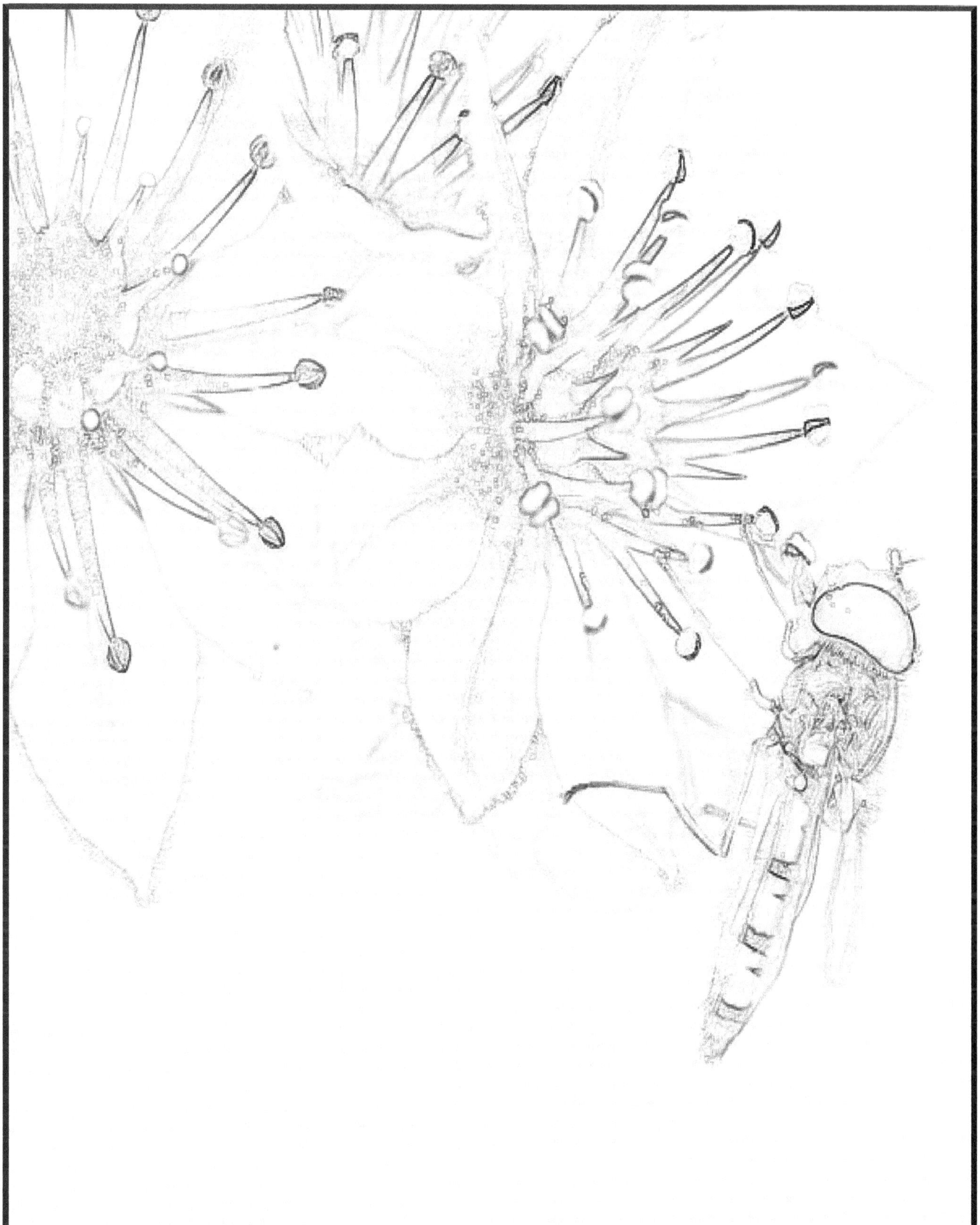

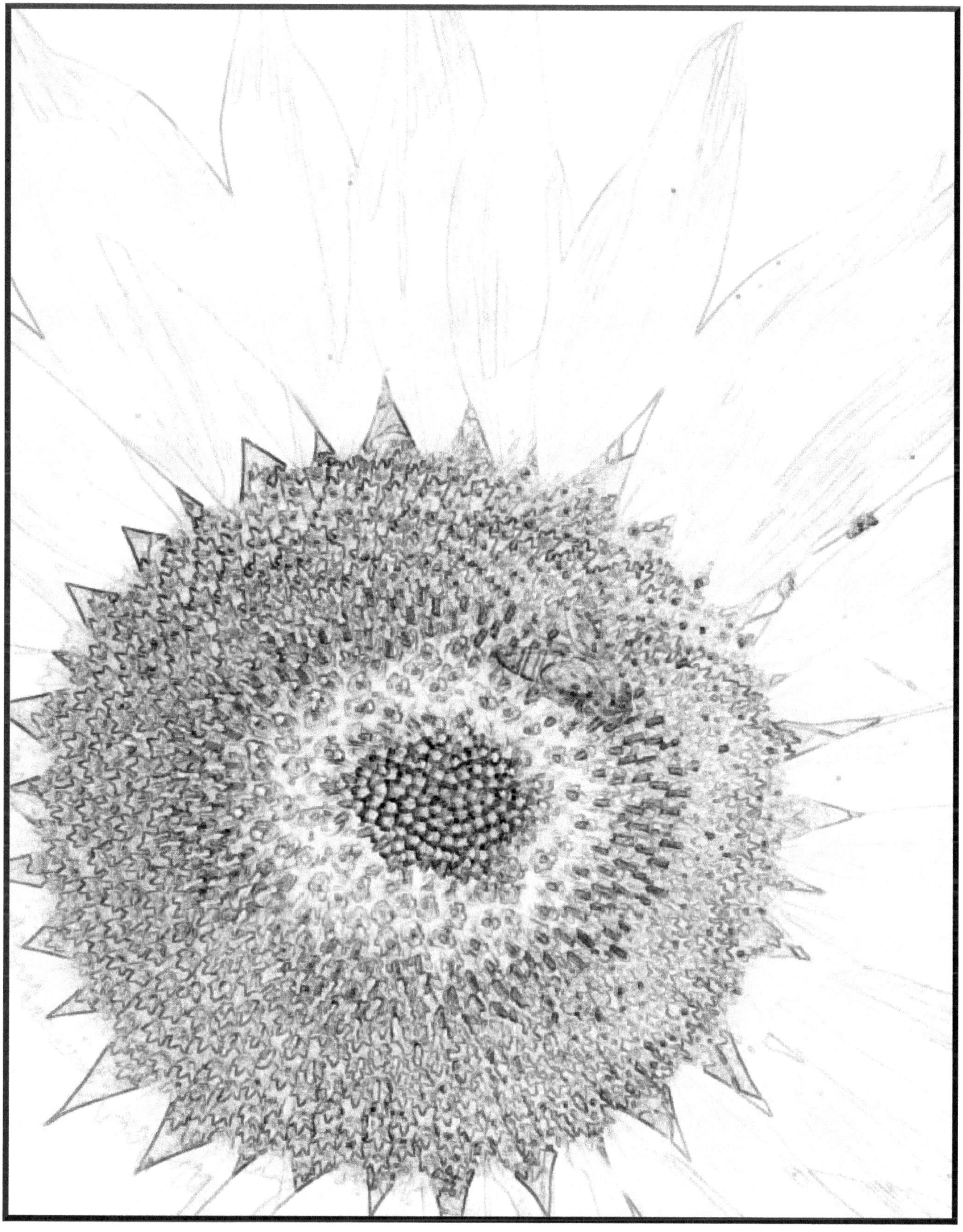

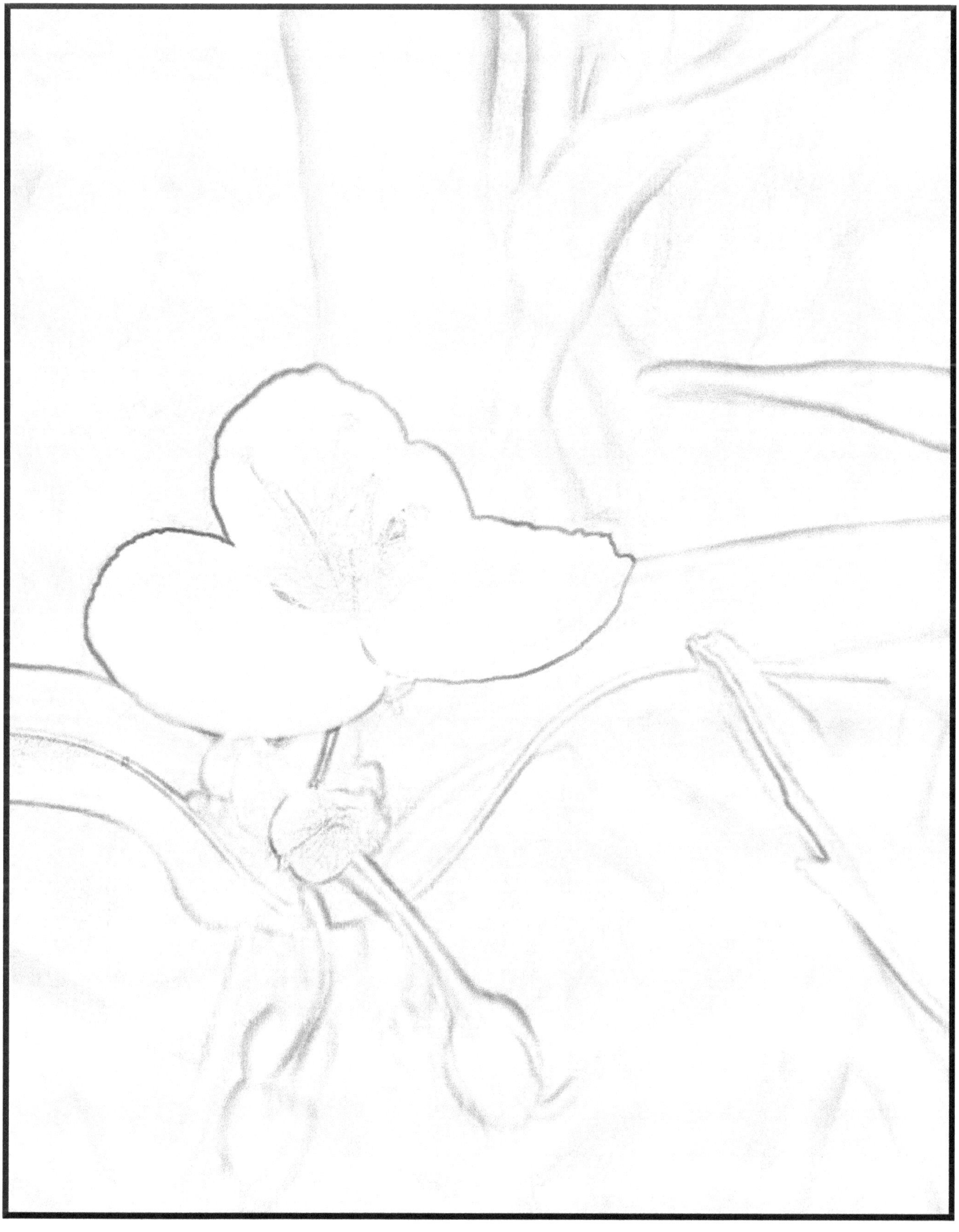

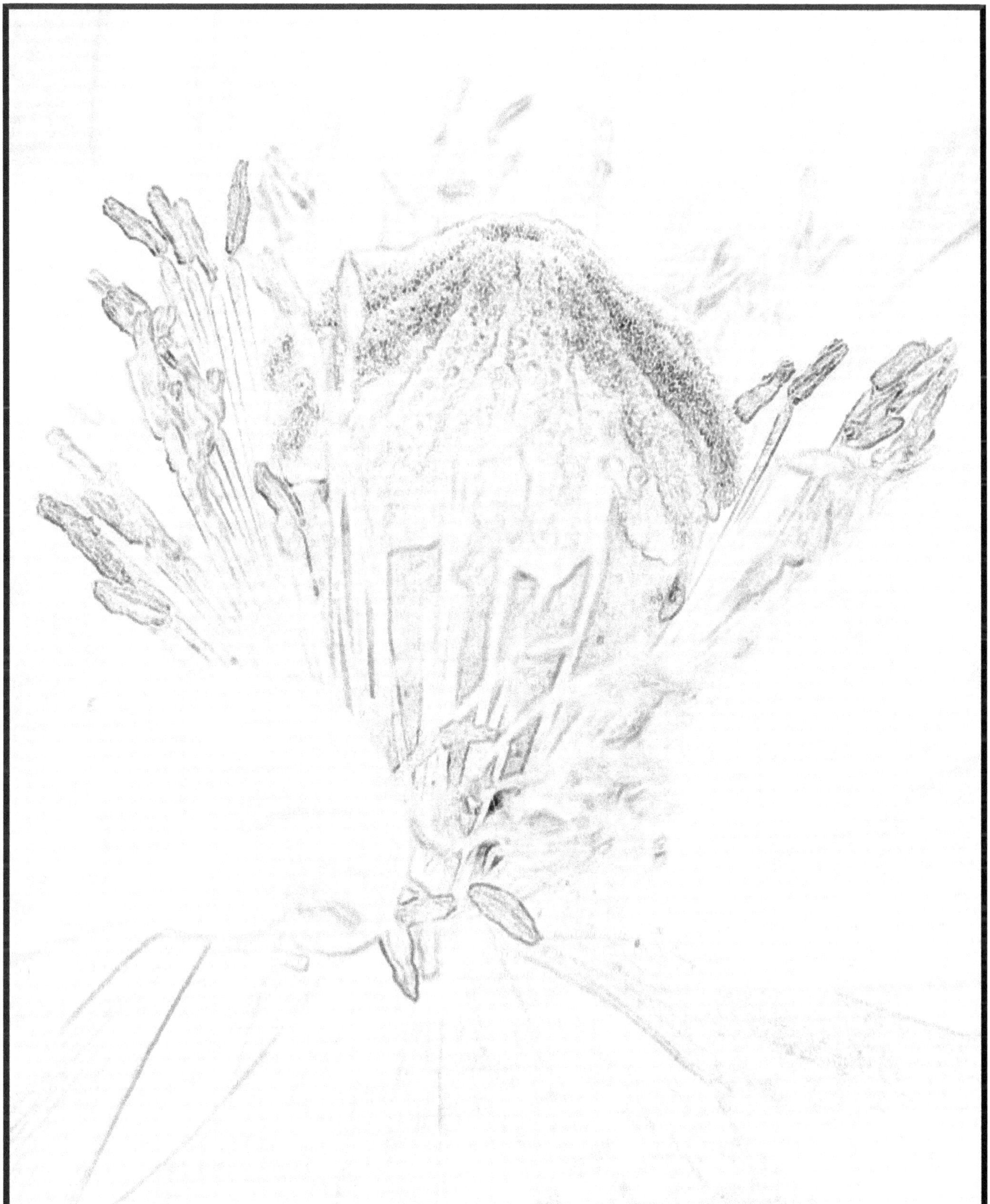

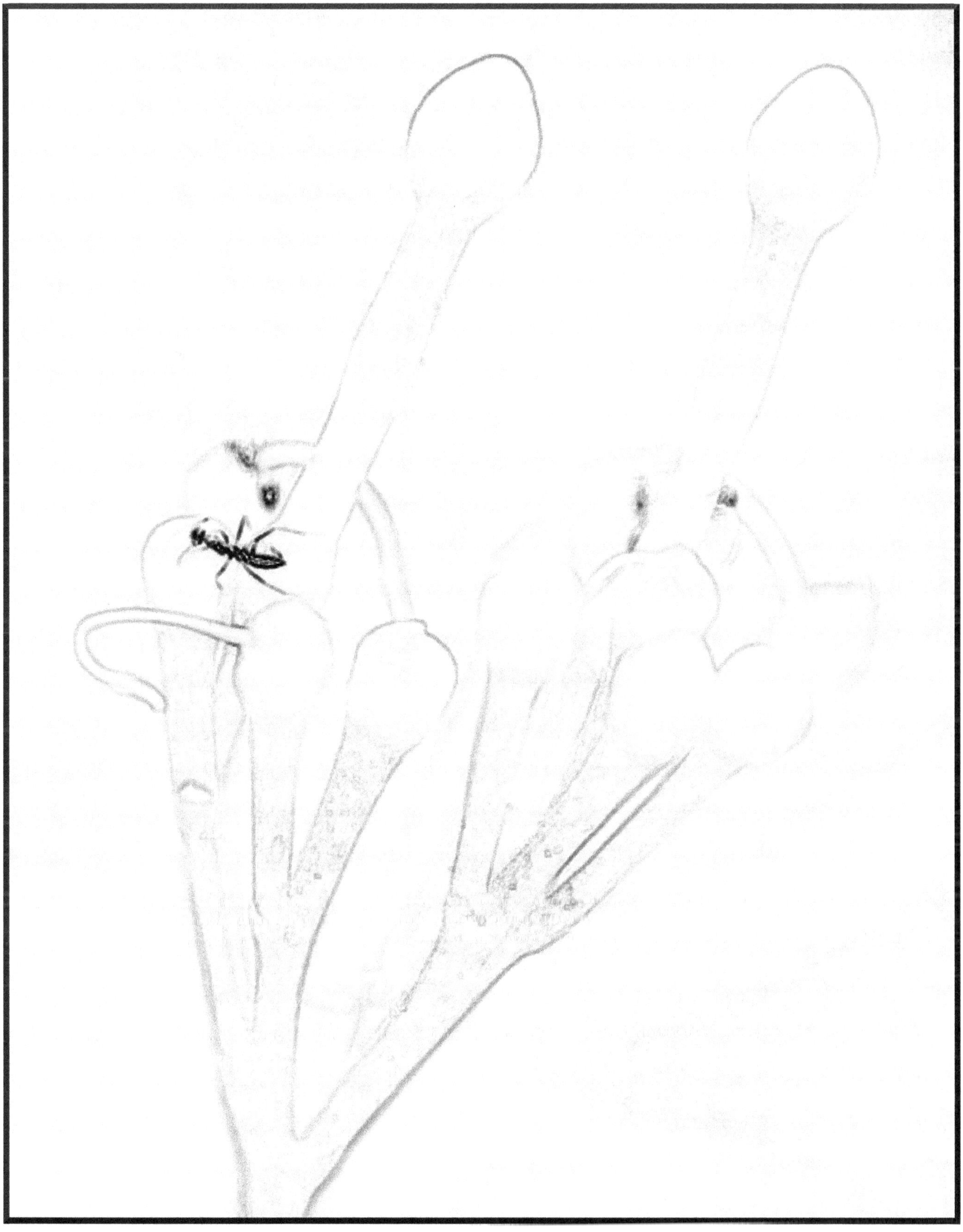

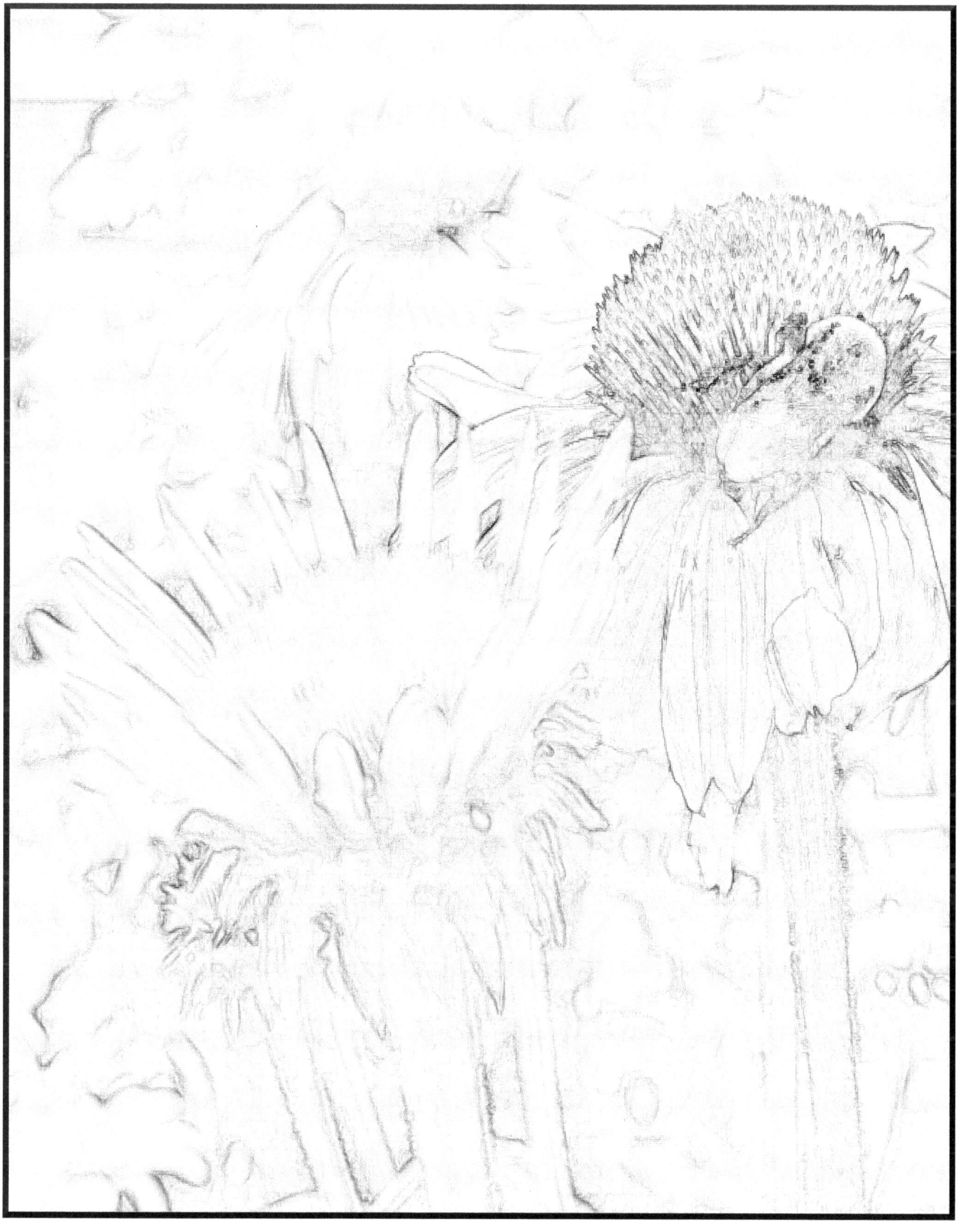

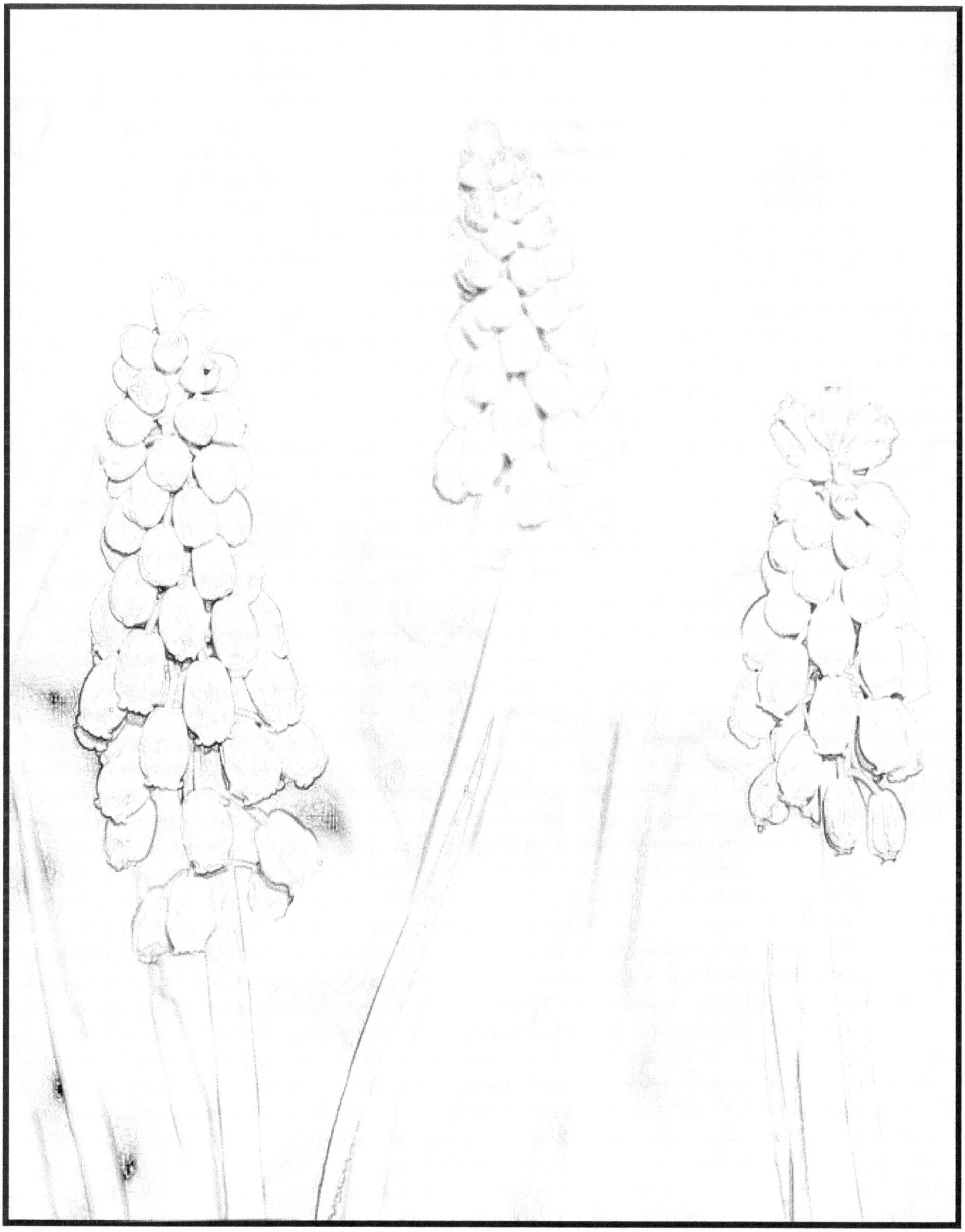

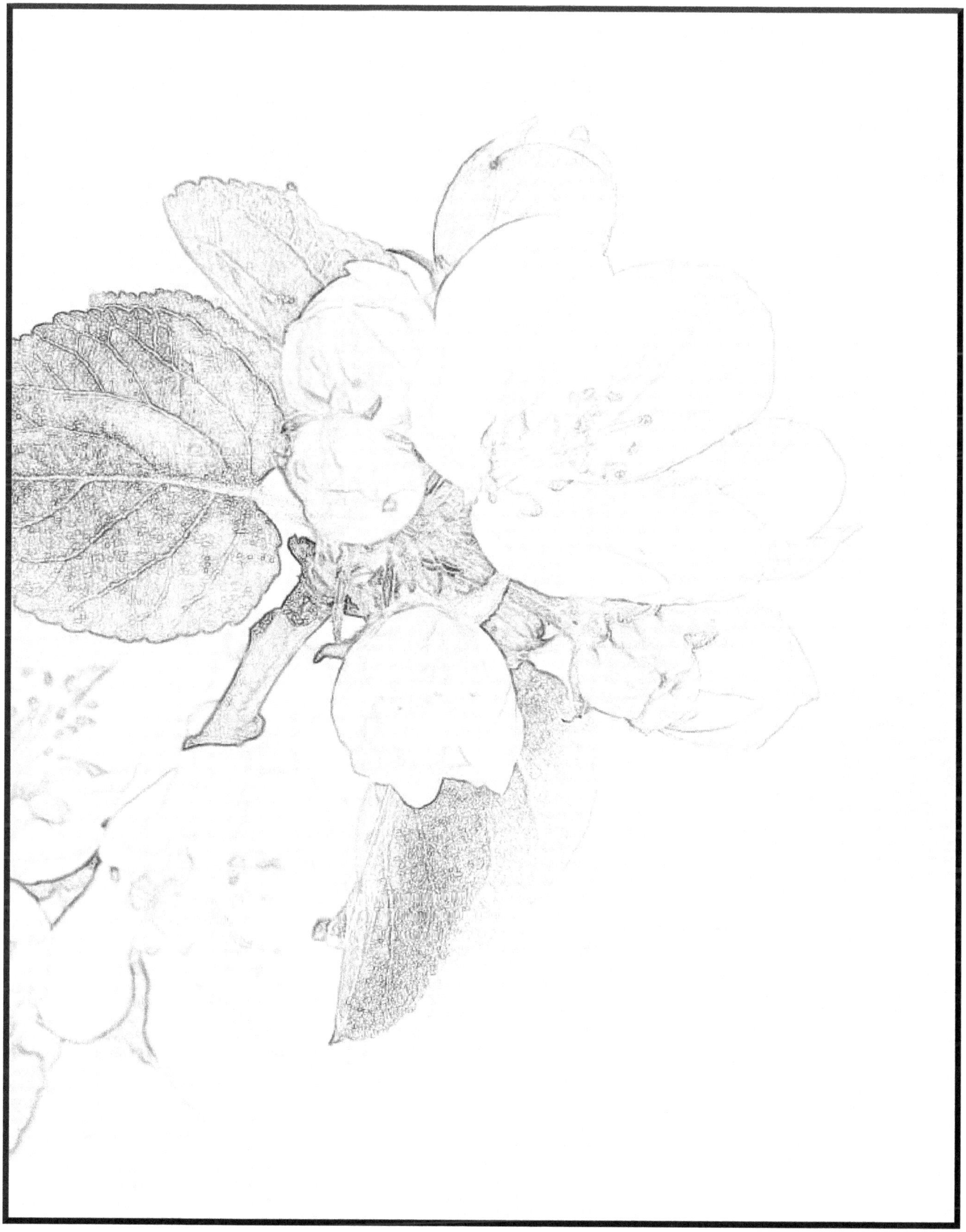

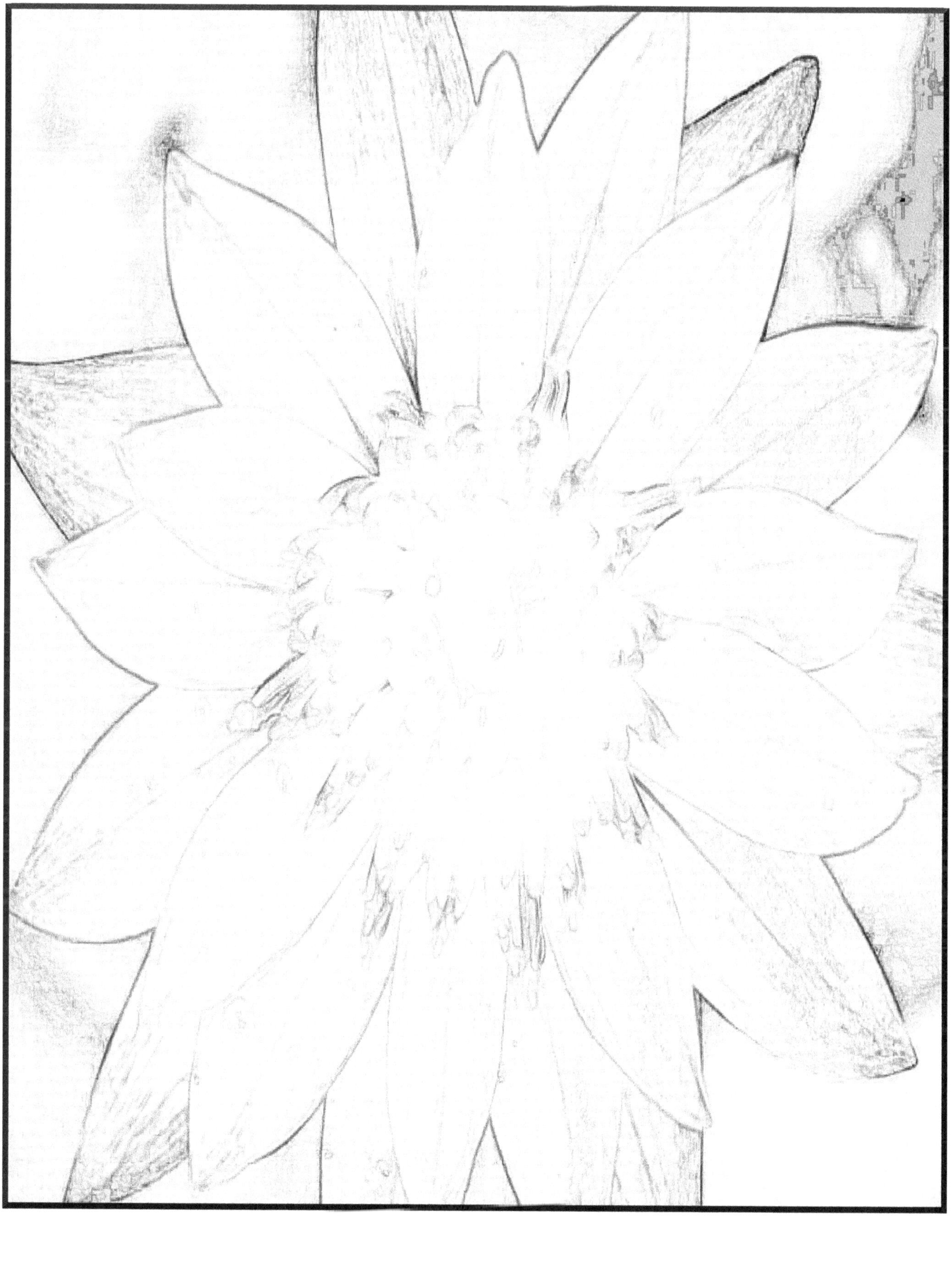

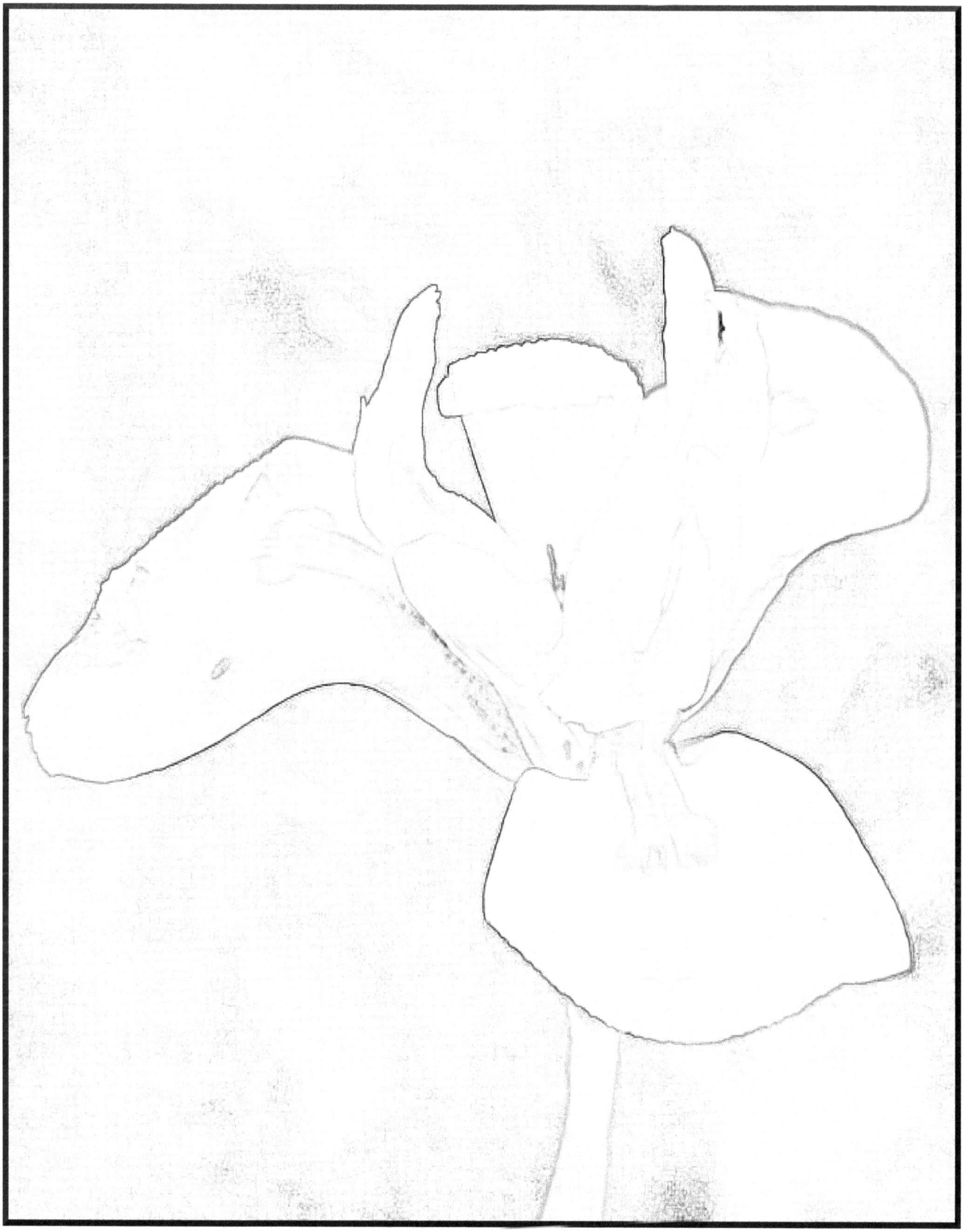

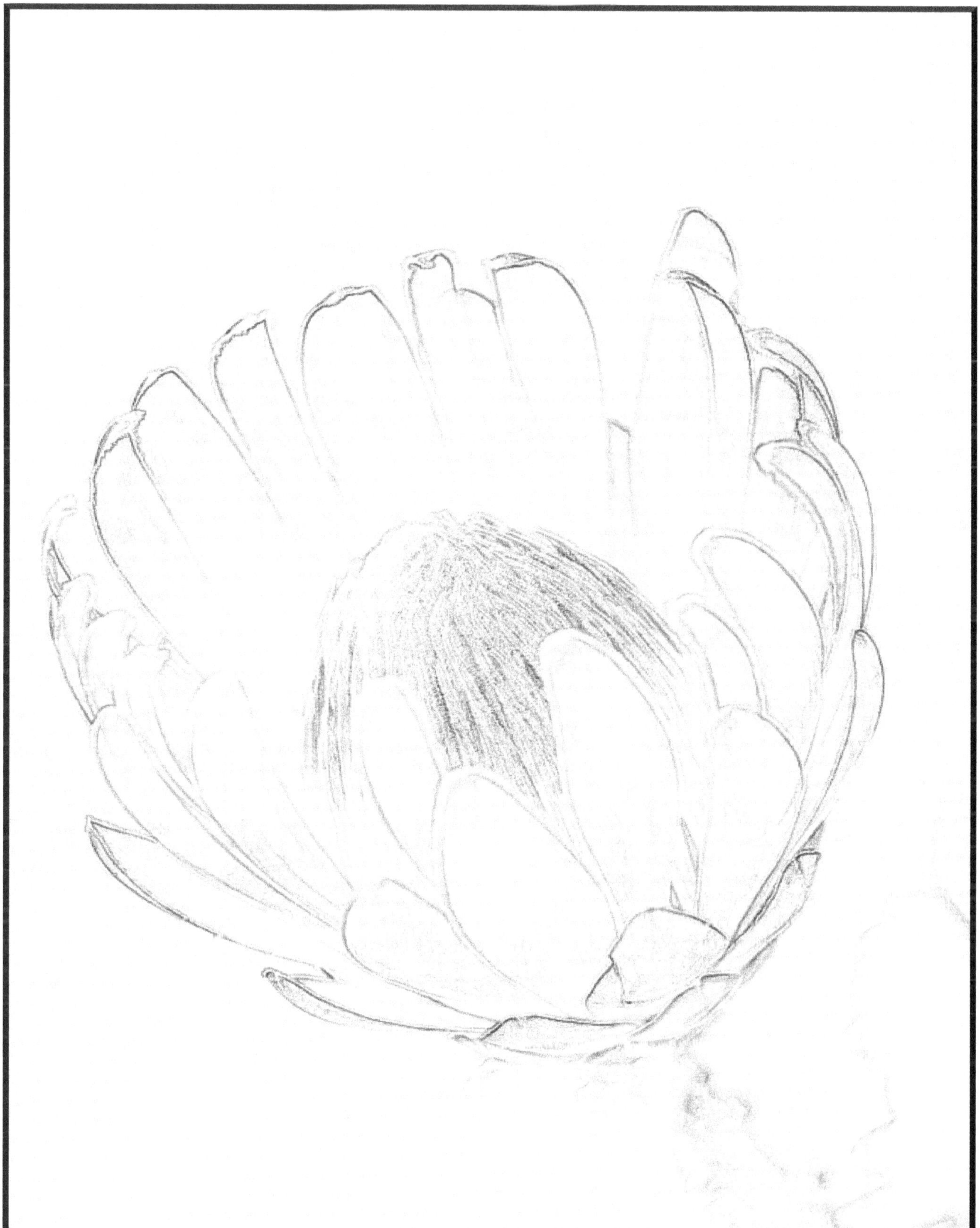

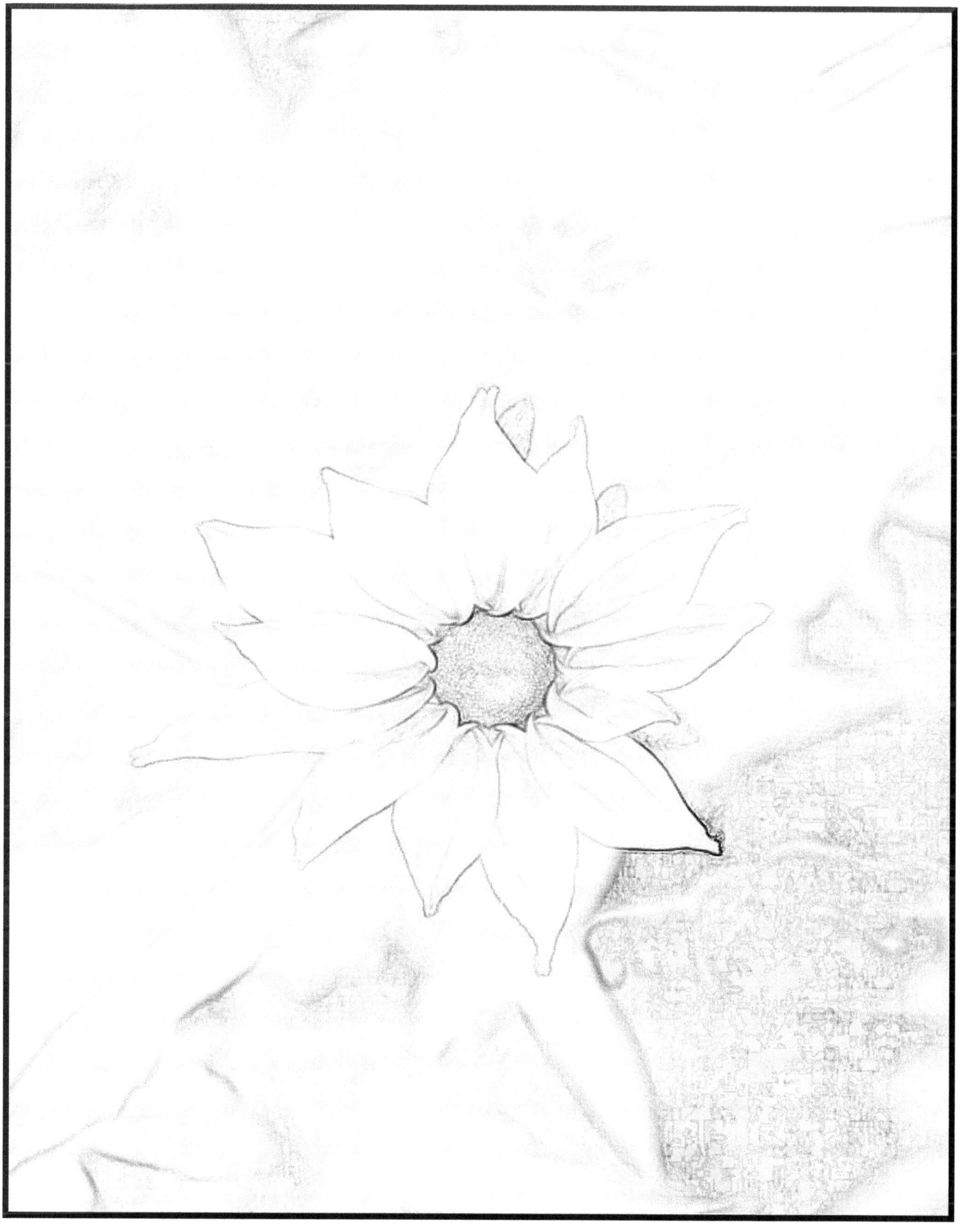

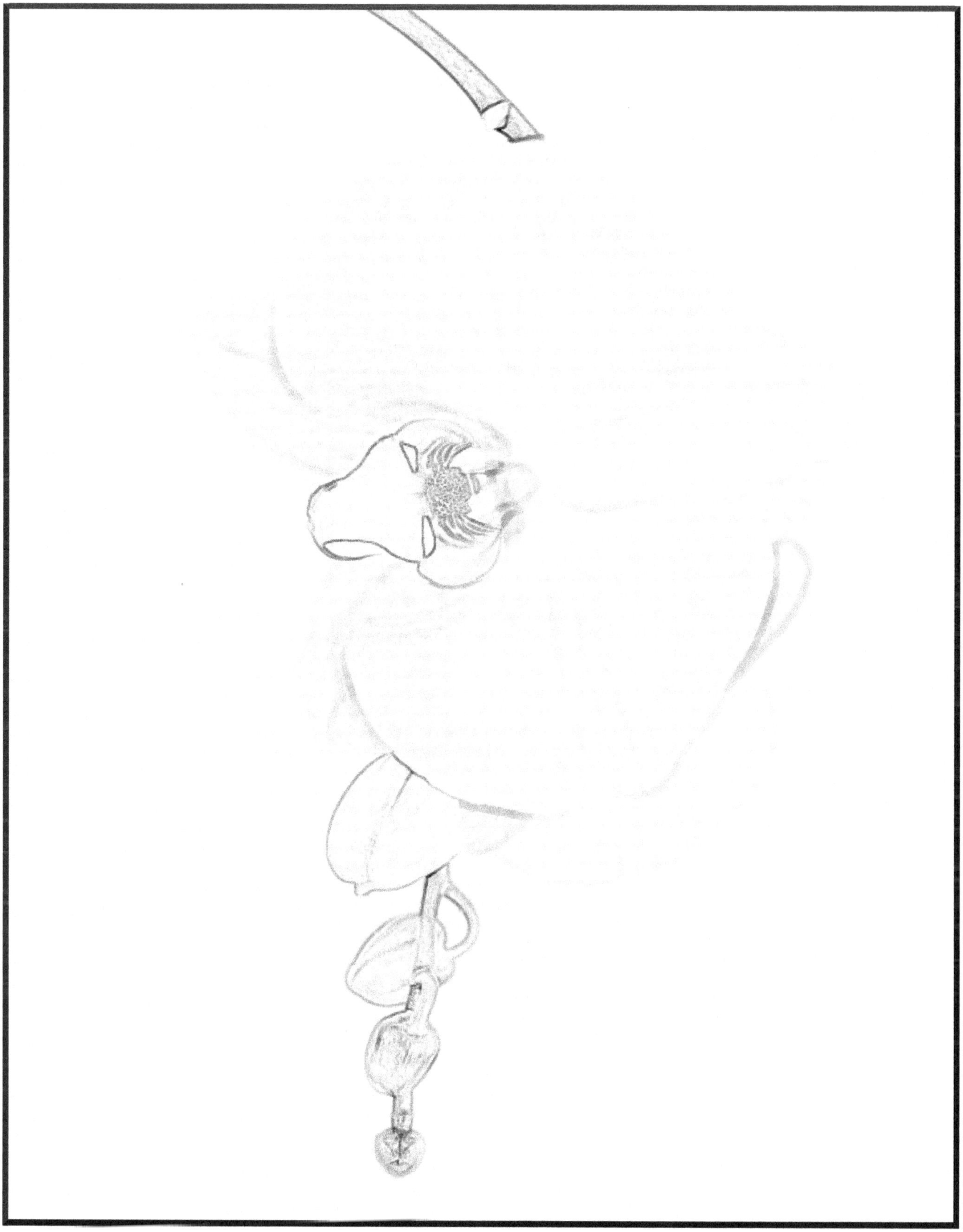

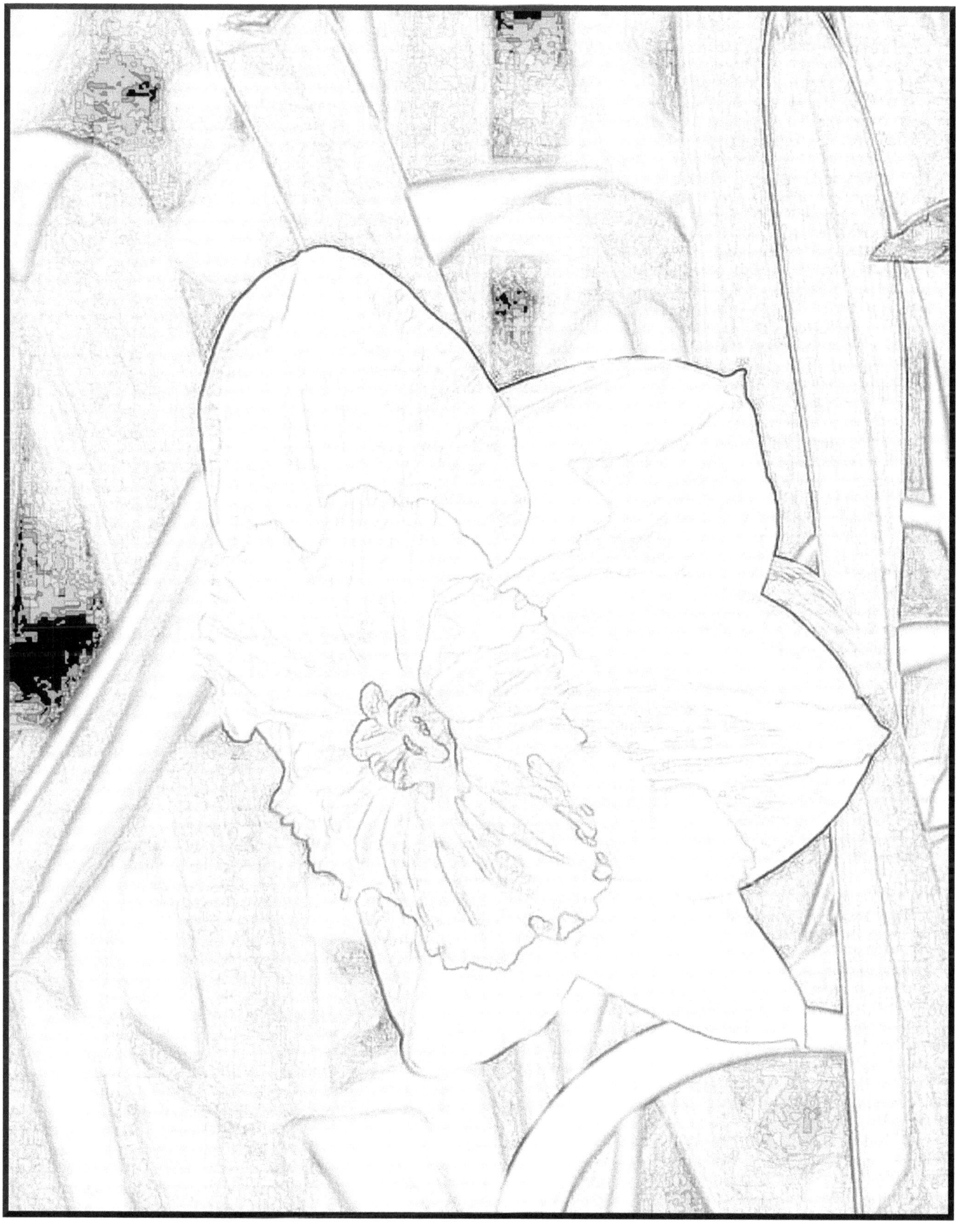

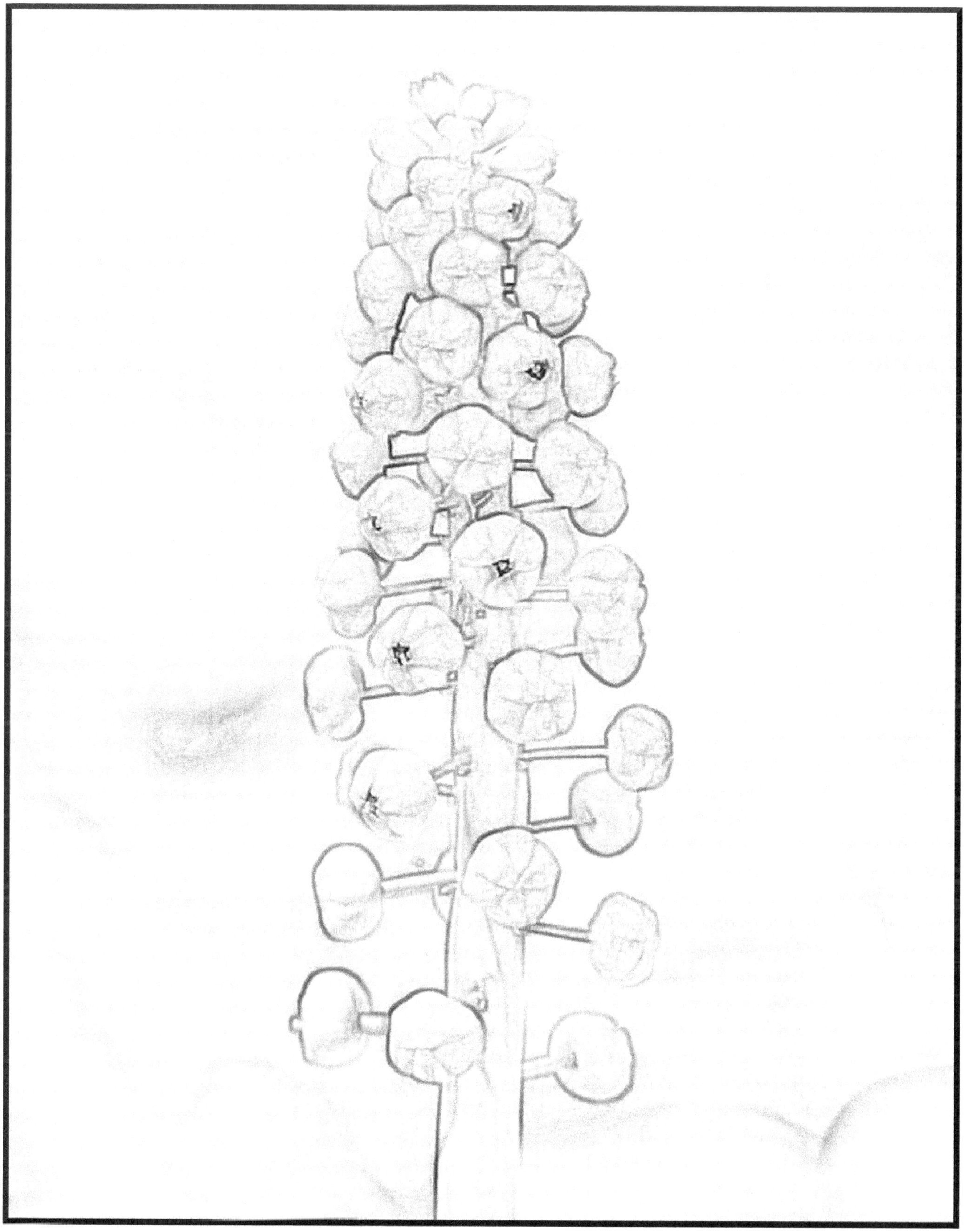

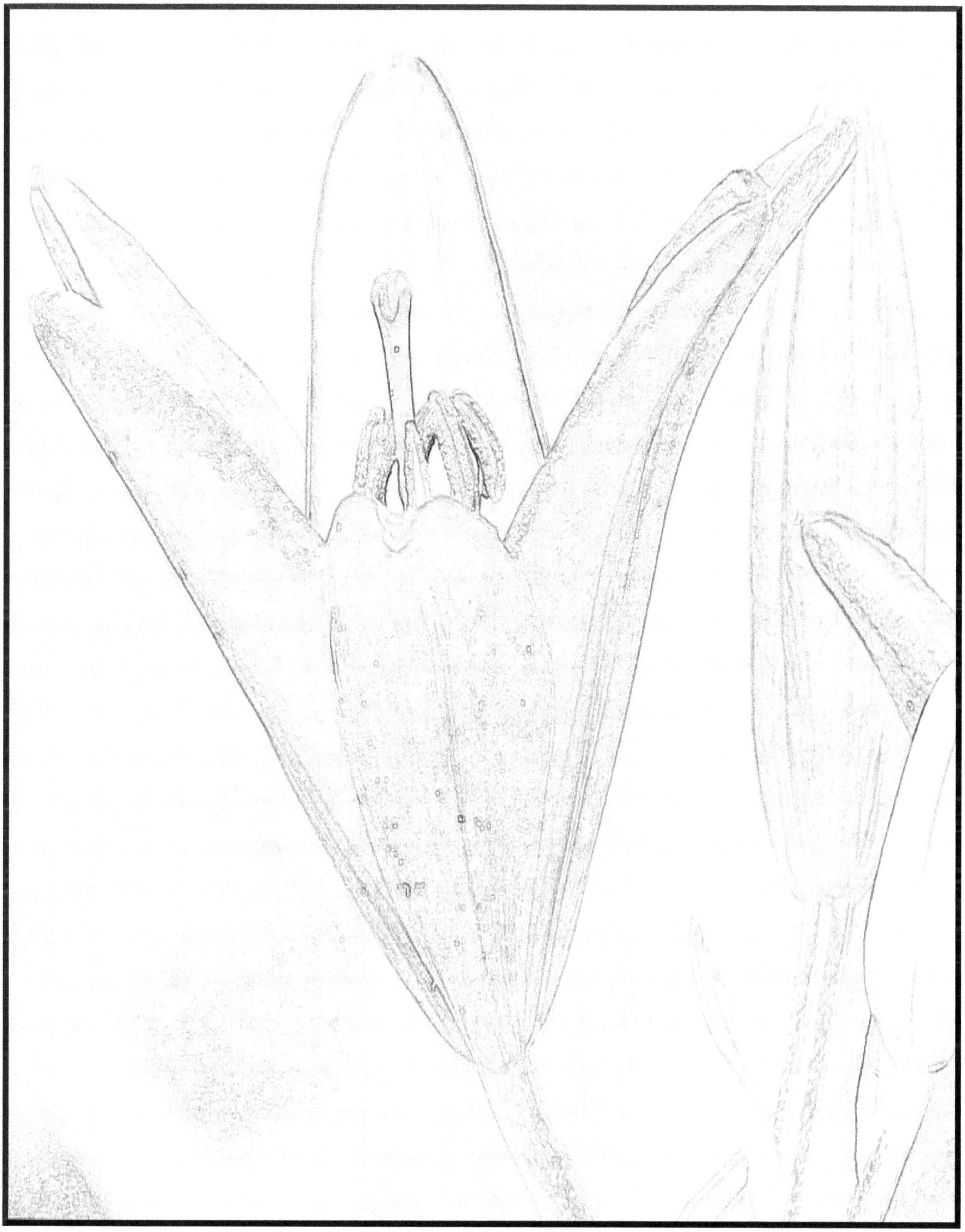

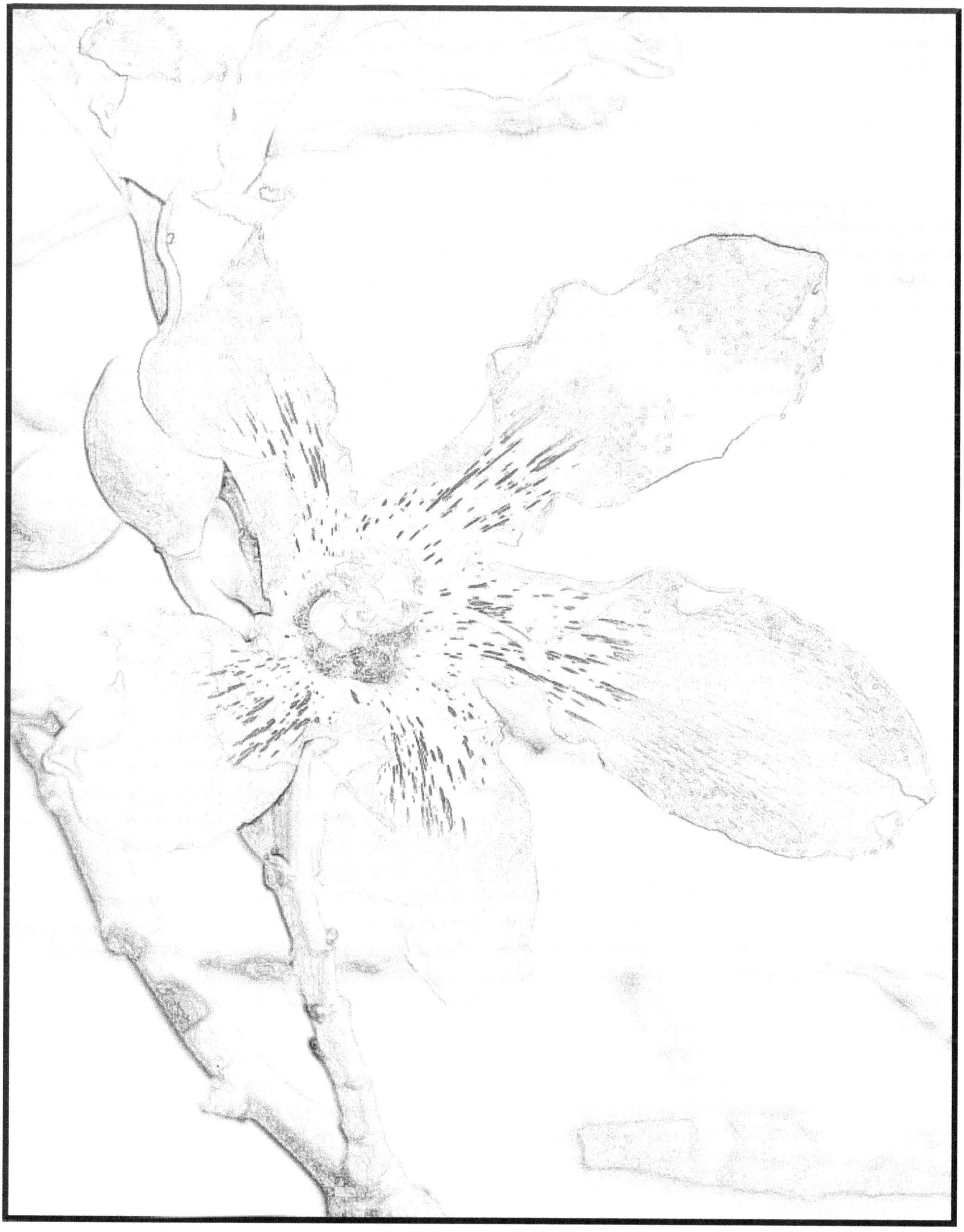

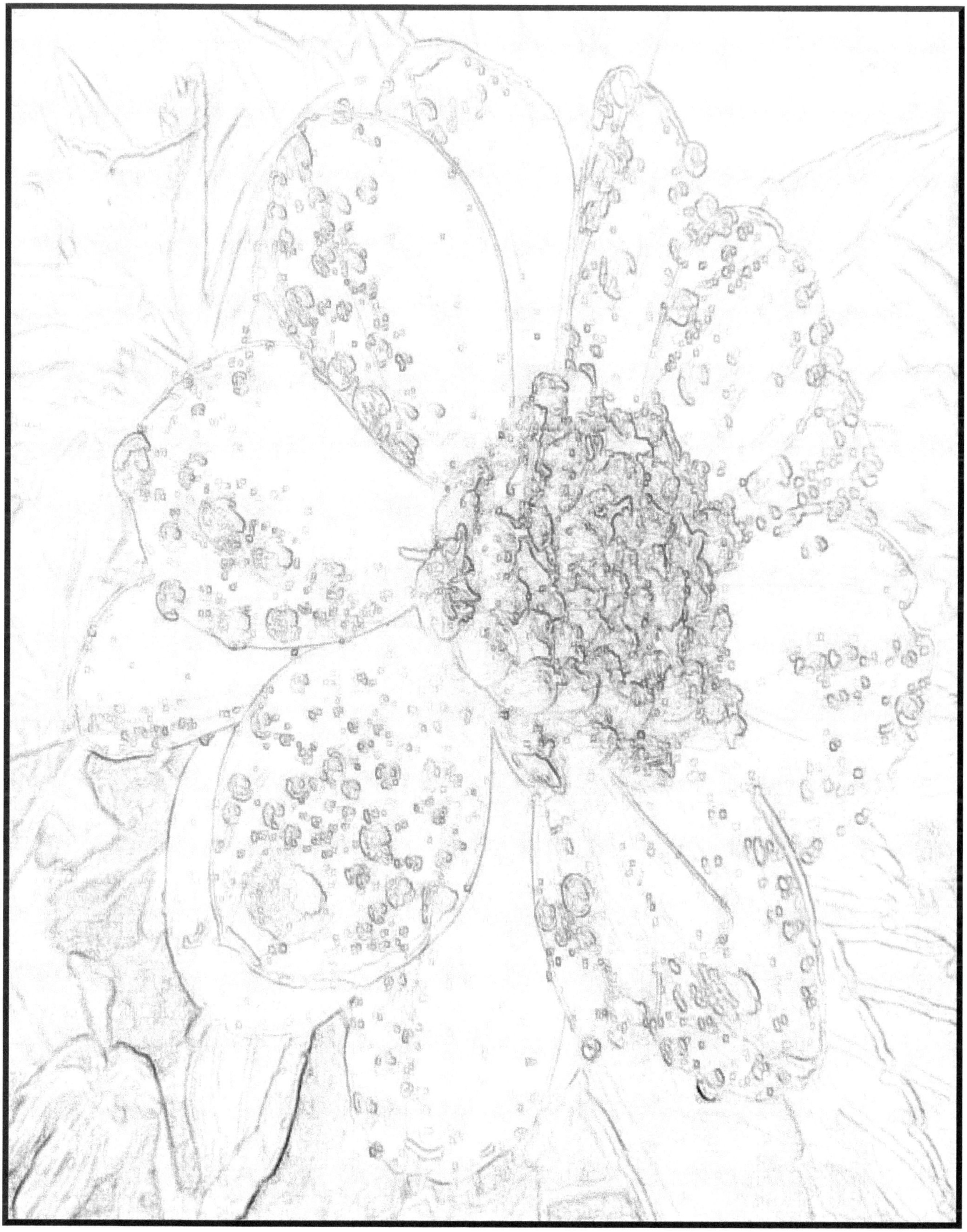

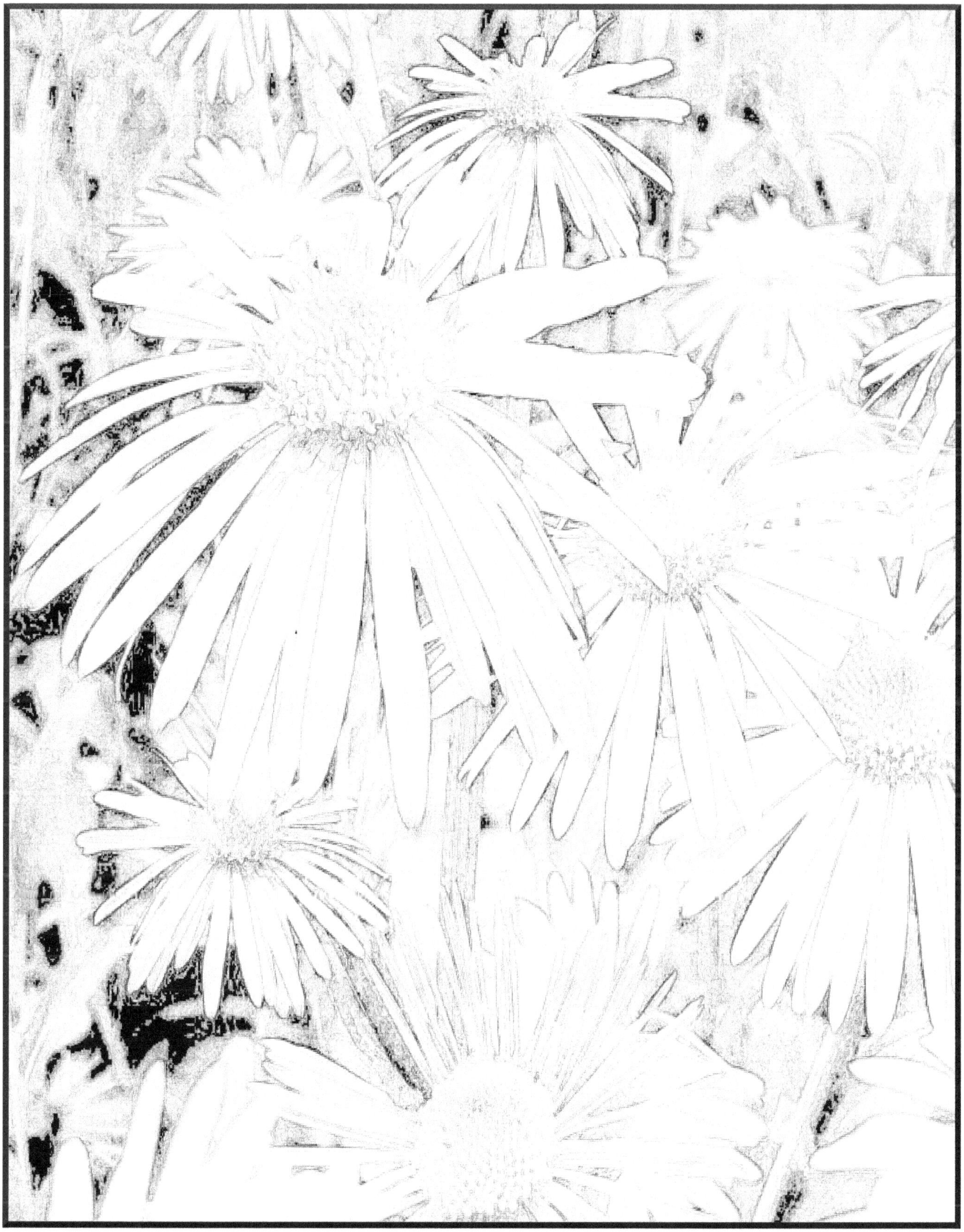

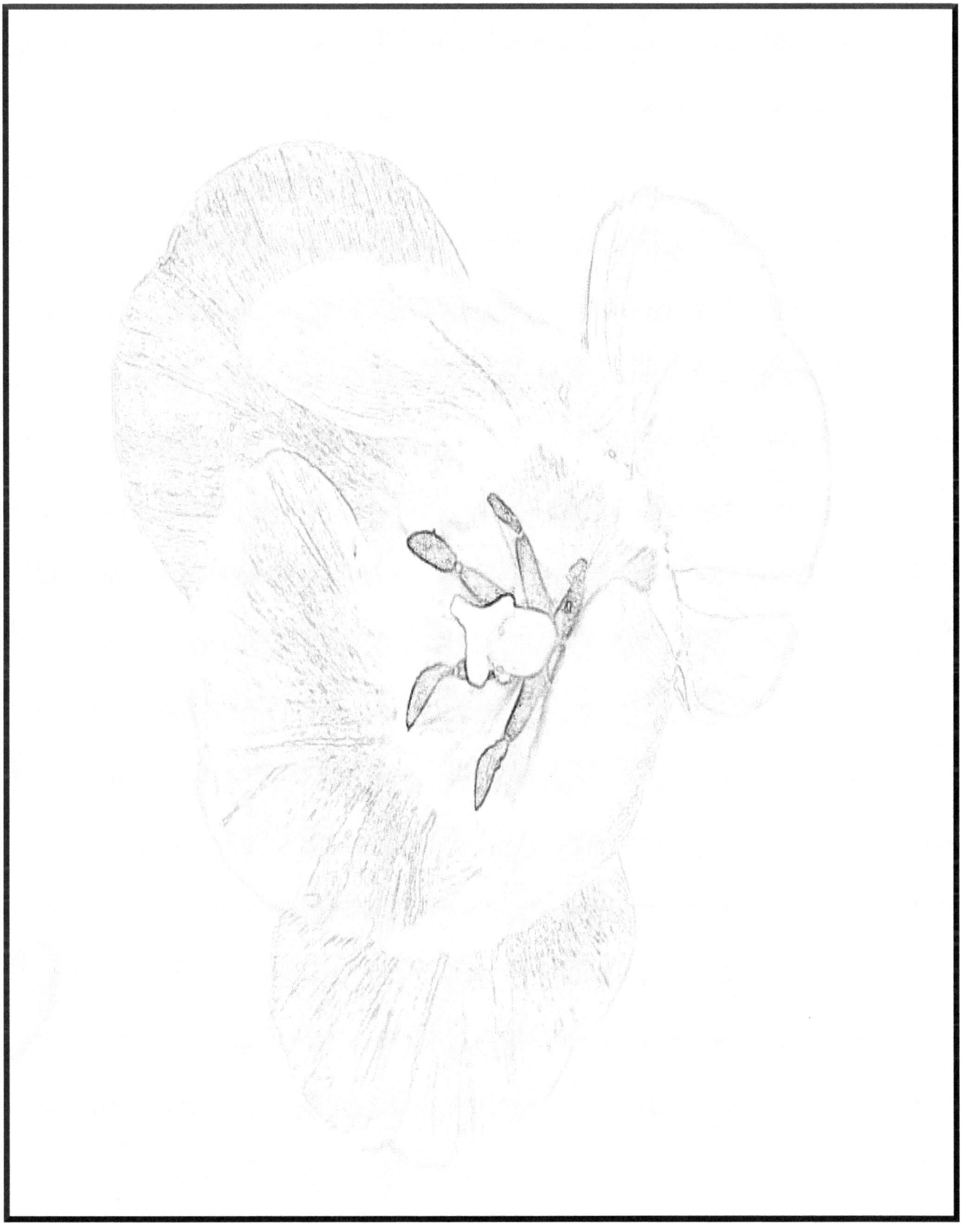

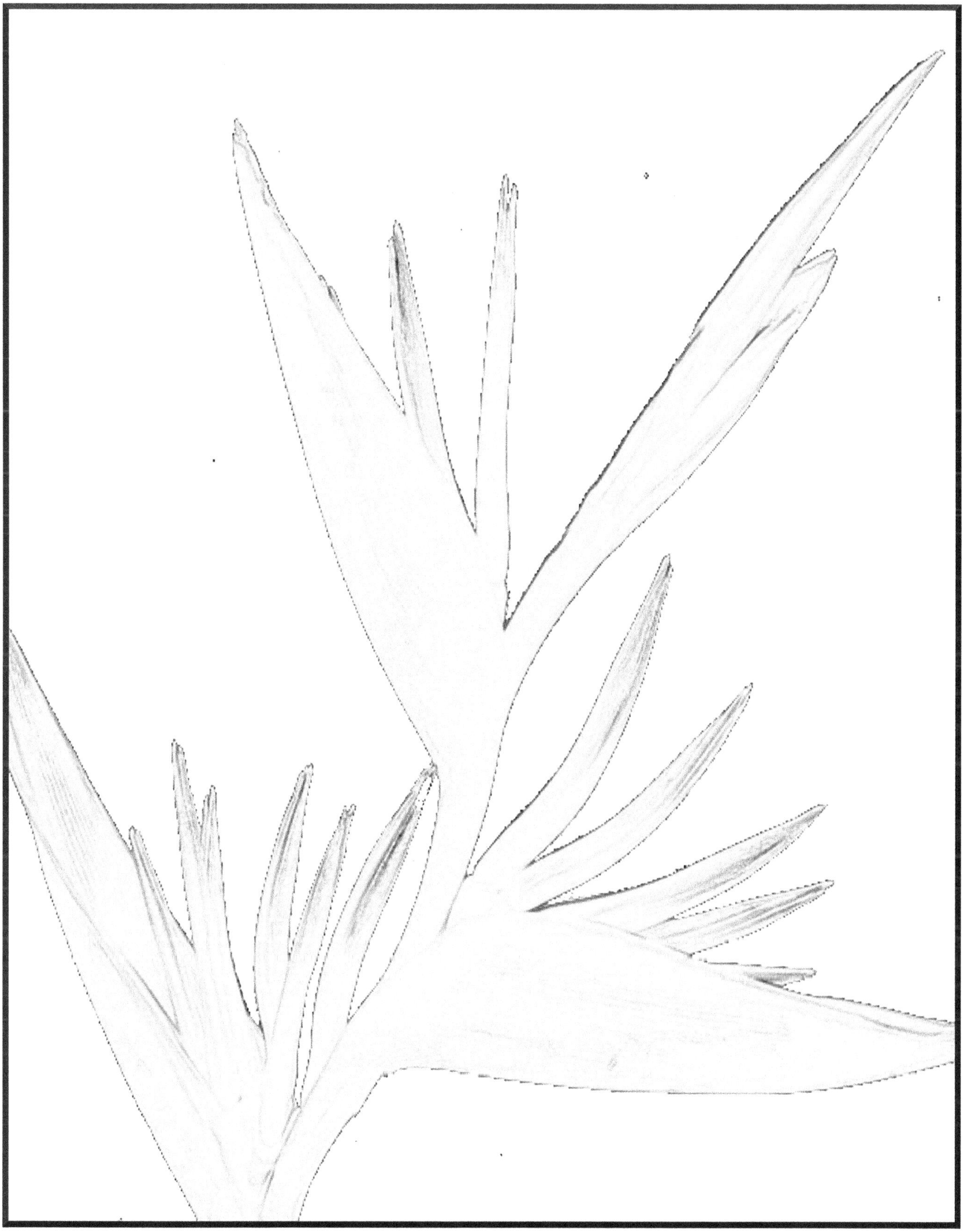

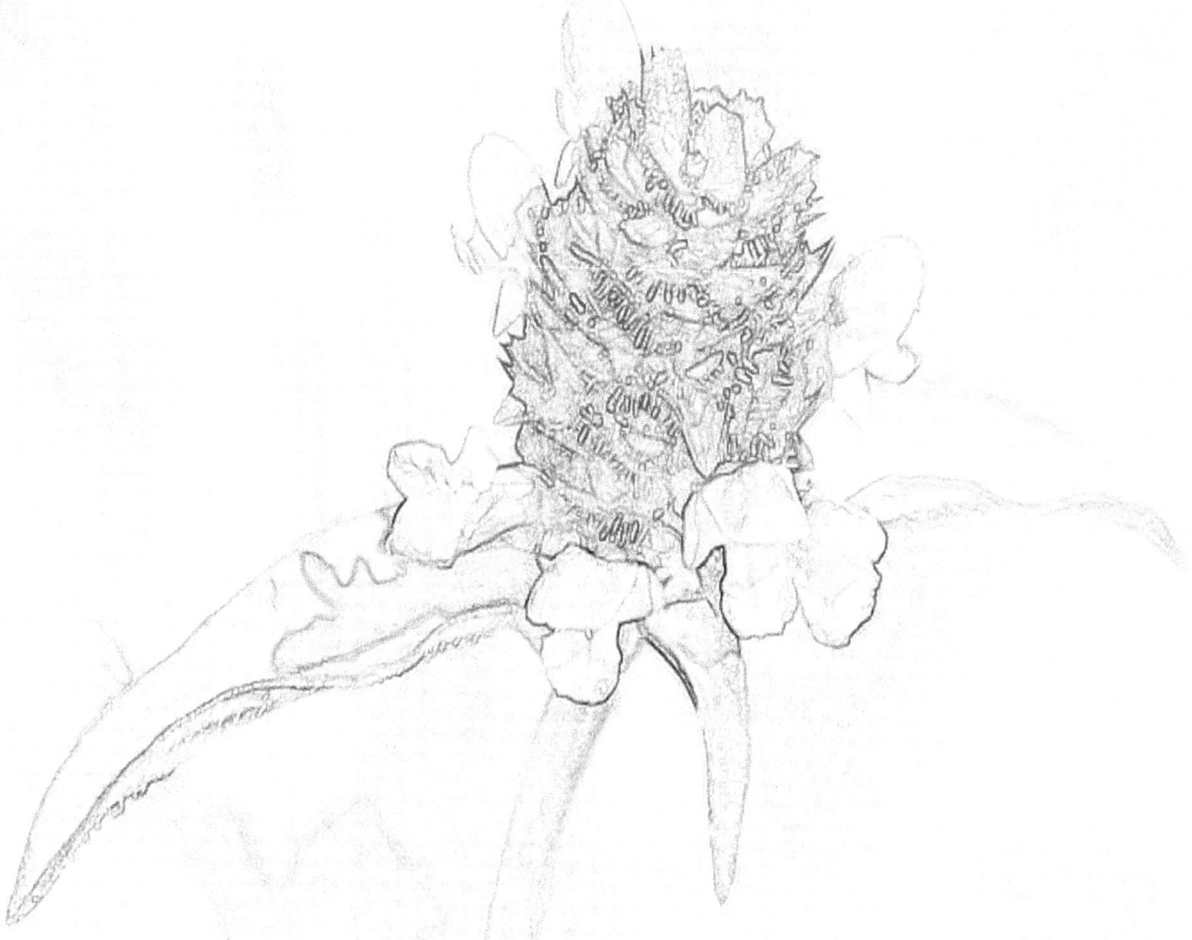

www.ingramcontent.com/pod-product-compliance
Lightning Source LLC
Chambersburg PA
CBHW081136170526
45165CB00008B/2693
* 9 7 8 1 5 4 8 3 5 9 7 8 2 *